Radical Spiritual Adventures - Everyday

For Inner Peace–Inspired
Creativity–Deep Happiness

Richard Lui
Jim Regan

Outskirts Press, Inc.
Denver, Colorado

Radical Spiritual Adventures - Everyday
For Inner Peace-Inspired Creativity-Deep Happiness

Outskirts Press, Inc.
http://www.outskirtspress.com

ISBN: 978-1-4327-5109-8

Outskirts Press and the "OP" logo are trademarks belonging to Outskirts Press, Inc.

PRINTED IN THE UNITED STATES OF AMERICA

Table of Contents

Acknowledgments

The authors wish to thank, first, the many other authors and teachers whose profound wisdom and insights contributed greatly to our understanding of life as adventure. We especially want to express our sincerest thanks and gratitude to Peter Campbell and Edwin McMahon, Kathlyn and Gay Hendricks, Paul McCormick, John Platt, and Gaylon Palmer who inspired us in so many untold ways on our own life's journey. Their work and devotion in the pursuit of personal growth and wellness, together with that of many unnamed others, is a gift beyond measure for which we are truly grateful.

We also want to acknowledge for their support and encouragement, our spouses Tamsen Taylor and Susan Burke, and family members Aaron, Allison and Megan Lui, and Richard's parents

Catherine and Ralph Lui. Collectively, their ideas and input have been invaluable in making this book possible.

Most books are not written solely by the authors alone. This book is no exception. It required a whole bunch of people to try to convert what we wrote into readable English. Because this book includes most all of the chapters of our first book, **Everyday Adventures** (that have been expanded and revised), plus the additional new chapters in this volume, major literary surgery was required. We very much wish to thank the following "surgeons" for their hard work: Mary Ann Baer, Diane Flood, Mary Pat Friar, Tracy Doolittle Gregory, Linda Haakenson, Fran Harrington, Sarah Holst and Paula Wakamiya.

Richard and Jim also wish to express our deep gratitude to our editor, Margaret Lambright. Margaret painstakingly revised our book with great skill, intuition, and incisive intelligence. Margaret is a kind and compassionate editor who we would recommend to anyone writing the book of their dreams.

Special thanks, in particular, also go to Carol Greenberg, Nancy Layton and Sue London of the Sacramento Learning Exchange, and Adele Hamlett and the staff of Sierra College Community Education. They have all contributed immensely to Richard's adult education classes over the years.

Most of all, we want to thank each other for making this collaborative effort an amazing adventure in itself. Our friendship and work together is a blessing in every sense of the word. We must also thank that invisible energy of love and compassion we call our Higher Power. It alone has provided the direction and led the way in preparing this book. We just listened and did the footwork.

Introduction

Everything about life is an adventure, and we can make everyday a radical spiritual adventure for inner peace, inspired creativity, deep happiness, and just ole lazy wandering and wondering, if we would only be open to experiencing it that way. The adventure begins with our willingness, our intent. Are we willing to experience each day as a profound sacred happening—a gift? Or are we judgmental, rigid and fearful, trying to control everything so that life will go perfectly and be how we think it should be? We can choose to be flexible, open to going with the flow, and become caught up in the joy of life's moment-to-moment adventure. It starts with our intent. And we can intend to live with this spirit of adventure.

Radical spiritual adventures are soulful, sacred,

deep-rooted happenings you can have every day if you are willing. Our use of the words "radical" and "spiritual" denote profound astonishing adventures you can have in your ordinary day-to-day living.

The definition of the word "radical" comes from what is essential or the root. Our sixteen radical spiritual adventures allow an unfolding to your essential or root wisdom. The word "spiritual", we use to describe adventures that take us to the sacred, an inner presence of peace, creativity, and guidance.

The practices in each chapter go beyond merely feeling our emotions. Simply knowing how you feel is only a beginning. We will invite you to embrace your feelings so they unfold to hidden felt senses or stories in your unconscious. Allowing these stories or felt meanings to release, opens us up to inner guidance, and felt shift to a calm center,

Our culture teaches us to control feelings, to try to fix them, or replace them with "better positive feelings" or even worse to numb our feelings, to get rid of them with substances, distractions, things, or other compulsions. Our culture teaches us to skip emotions and their felt meanings and thus repress our essential sacred rootedness. Our sixteen internal and external adventures will allow you to open to your true self, your inner wonder child of authentic experience which can include emotions, needs, felt meanings, grief and loss as well as joy and enthusiasm.

An example of one inner radical adventure is a

client of Richard's, a highly successful but suffering workaholic. David (not real name) received a diagnosis of cancer in his early 50's after a life of driving himself at work with little play or fun. David, after recovering from cancer, made a decision to slow his hurried and harried pace. He learned spiritual tools to listen deeply to his bodies emotions and sensations and uncovered a fear of failure and perfectionism learned as a small child. He embraced this fear and it released to inner wisdom guiding him that he was enough just being. From this connection to his true self he was guided to more play and creativity and balance. He started acting classes at his local community theater and cutback on his work schedule. He opened to a balanced life at work, play, and creativity. David (now in his 60's) and cancer free used many of the inner adventures in our book to surrender to inner wisdom in his own body for inner peace and guidance.

That's what this book is about and more. It is the product of an adventure of two friends—Richard and Jim—exploring the joy of adventure itself as a way to experience deeper happiness. Our vision is to give you practical spiritual tools to unleash your body's wisdom by sharing our experiences and observations on how to expand your sense of adventure and aliveness in your everyday life.

We want your journey to a more adventurous everyday life to be an adventure in itself. Start with a topic that most intrigues you or go in the order that appears in this book. It's up to you. Our book is a collection of contemplative adventures as well as exciting, action-oriented adventures. Do them in whatever order you wish. Do as many as you wish. Each one will take you deeper and deeper into more joy, peace and creativity while allowing a compassionate, gentle release of tension and stress.

We selected these deeply joyful adventures on the basis of them being the most practical and profound adventures that anyone can integrate into an already busy life. Our book is not only about how to improve your occasional vacation adventures, but also about bringing a sense of adventure into **each** day of your life. We believe our book will give you more practical spiritual tools for deep happiness than many of the other "happy books" on the shelf of your library or bookstore.

Now you may ask, "How can I have more excitement and joy and fun in my life with all my obligations, children to raise, bills to pay, etc.?"

By slowly integrating the Basic Principles and using some of the guidelines provided in the following pages, you will expand your sense of awe and wonder. And—we wish for all of you—to find through these adventures many paths to deeper meaning and profound happiness.

The Basic Principles of Radical Spiritual Adventuring

1. Life is an adventure in and of itself. You can try to remain a spectator of life, but eventually you may

be swept up by the essential adventures that life provides whether you like it or not.

2. Spiritual adventuring refers to connecting to intuitive body wisdom that is available to help and guide our lives every moment to peace and joy. It is not about trying to fix or avoid or analyze our feelings. It is about caring for our emotions and sensations so they can reveal divine gifts. It may or may not include religious beliefs or concepts. Spirituality is not necessarily the same as religious doctrine. Spirituality is based on a body experience that leads to ease and insight.

3. Life as adventure is bold, uncertain and a sometimes risky undertaking. It is an exciting experience—we are all adventurers in this venture of life. It becomes safe when we connect to a caring, feeling Presence or "inner loving allies" (usually a small number people we actually know or, more likely, people we know about who are alive now or lived hundreds or thousands of years ago) and who we believe would understand, totally accept, approve and support us in every possible way just as we are today plus would know exactly how to gently and lovingly support us to make any changes that would give us even more of that which we are truly searching for which hasn't yet occurred to us.

4. Spiritual adventuring is an attitude of living in the moment and being open to wonder, as well as to the awe and beauty that is all around us.

5. Our future dreams of adventure keep us more fully alive in the present. These dreams draw

us to our passions and creativity which are our gifts to ourselves and humanity.

6. Adventuring with the ordinary aspects of our lives, i.e. our daily living, can awaken us to the gifts of each moment.

7. Adventuring with the adversity of tough times can be the highest form of adventure. Life is at times unfair and sends us challenging tests. The adventure is to find the sometimes hidden blessing in what seems on the surface to be a negative event.

8. There are two kinds of adventures: Internal or inner adventures of the heart and spirit and outer adventures with creativity in our environment. Mastering the art of both types of adventuring is a lifetime process.

9. Adventure doesn't require focusing on a particular outcome. Enjoy the process and the outcome will take care of itself.

10. Radical spiritual adventures are fundamental, intuitive adventures of the heart. We become more excited and alive and yet have a core of stillness and serenity.

11. Radical spiritual adventuring occasionally invites a day of spontaneous wandering, a freedom to just meander, putter around, be childlike with complete permission to produce nothing and go nowhere in particular. This day of imagination and reverie allows rest and openness to creativity and renewal. No more doing, doing, doing—just being, being, being.

Practicing Adventure as a Path to Happiness

Now that we've highlighted the principles, here are some ideas for acting on the intention of living with more adventure.

1. Make a commitment to expand your spirit of adventure a little each week with patience and compassion.

2. In the beginning, start with small adventures of five minutes per day—doing either inner or outer adventures.

3. Plan adventures by yourself, with a friend, or in a small group. Discover by experimenting whether solo adventuring or adventuring with one or more people is best for you.

4. Some people benefit from using a journal to write down adventures—their own private adventure journal.

5. Start with outer adventures and move to inner adventures. Feel free to skip any that may not appeal to you, or try them in any sequence you like. This is **your** adventure.

6. Try one or more experiences in each chapter for the most benefit. Finding a daily practice is the key for learning. Start a support group of two or more kindred spirits to help you on this journey.

7. Acknowledge, but don't believe, your resistance or internal critic. Your critic may come up to sabotage the joy of adventuring. We all have old self-critical tapes which might say:

- "I'm too old for this adventure stuff."
- "I don't deserve to feel happy."
- "I haven't enough time, energy, or money to do these adventures."
- "Adventures are just for my once-a-year vacation."
- "This is too risky and scary. I'll get hurt."

You will be given many tools—especially to embrace and release the critic. Naming and unmasking the critic, not fighting it, is a good first step. The critic part of you is simply afraid and needs reassurance from your own compassion and love. Other internal and external allies of your adventuring spirit can help you with shrinking your critic. Use one of these allies to help counter the old critic tapes above. Start out with a set of intensions and use the tools in our chapters to manifest them:

I can adventure at any age. I will find role models of adventurers in my age group. Age is not a factor.

I have a right to feel happy in my life. I can claim my right to dream and take adventures big and small.

I can start a little at a time by taking only five to ten minutes each day for creating adventure. I can make the time and prioritize a day where adventure is part of my experience.

Life is an adventure already. Vacations are only one kind of adventure.
I can create safe, small adventures by myself or with a buddy. And I will do only what I am ready to do, by taking baby steps.

Now, On To The Journey!

"Our life is frittered away
  by detail...
Simplify, Simplify."

— Henry David Thoreau

CHAPTER **1**

Daily Adventures and Radical Spiritual Rewards —

Growing Where You Are Planted

Though we may not specifically be aware of it, there is plenty of evidence to suggest that we are actually starving for a greater degree of adventure in our normal, day-to-day lives. Even if we subconsciously concluded a long time ago that having an adventurous daily life wasn't very realistic or feasible, our hunger for it is still quite evident.

The immense popularity, in the past decade, of the sports utility vehicle is, no doubt, one obvious example of our longing for a greater sense of adventure. The huge popularity of sophisticated tactical computer games may just be another example of this hunger for excitement missing in our everyday existence. The success of the big-budget action thrillers at the movies suggests the same need. Even the interest in such things as aromatherapy, scented candles, fragrant lotions and exotic-smelling bath products may have to do with wanting to bring more adventure to our physical senses. All of this provides evidence to suggest we are truly craving more refreshing, invigorating and enriching experiences that many of us now find lacking in our ordinary day-to-day lives.

So how do we begin to satisfy this appetite for a more intriguing, interesting and adventurous everyday life?

Change Expectations

The first thing we can do to bring greater adventure into our daily lives is to change some of our rigid situational expectations. It is not uncommon to rush through our day expecting everything to go smoothly. We like things to be as simple as possible. We dislike complications and disruptions. We want things to be more or less predictable, with few surprises to upset us.

An amazing thing happens when we stop expecting things to generally be as we think they "should" be. An amazing thing happens when we no longer view specific events of our day as good or bad, or as right or wrong. An amazing thing happens when we expand our black and white situational expectations to allow a multitude of daily events and circumstances to be not only acceptable but even intriguing. Everything seems to go more smoothly, and everything seems to become easier. It's a paradox.

Best of all, once we stop "shoulding" on the particulars of our day—once we stop expecting things to go right—things seem to stop going wrong as often. As we switch from wanting everything to go as planned, to be uneventful, we discover that every moment of every day can be an amusing, amazing, fascinating, colorful, on-going adventure.

Practice: *Transforming Our Daily Expectations*

Here are a few things I find helpful in changing rigid, stress-producing, anxiety-prone, adventure-limiting expectations.

   — On my desk and in my car I keep a couple of 3"x5" cards on which I have written the slogan, "LIFE IS WHAT HAPPENS WHEN YOU ARE MAKING OTHER PLANS." Besides glancing at this slogan every so often, I read it aloud to myself as soon as I become aware that my narrow expectations are beginning to limit my openness to being spontaneous in the here and now.

   — I loosely group the things I expect to do in a day into two-hour segments and include in each of these segments approximately thirty minutes for delays and interruptions. This allows me to experience the disruptions throughout the day as part of that day's adventure instead of just more hassles in my life.

Stretch Time

Another way we can create more adventure in everyday life is to stretch our time. Believe it or not, time is elastic. There is a way to stretch time whenever we want. Here's how it works.

When we are in a hurry and are trying to get everything done as quickly as possible, time contracts. The faster we go, the less time we have. On the other hand, when we're ahead of schedule and in no real hurry, time sort of expands, and we end up getting more done than we expected.

It's amazing how this works. It's another paradox. This incredible phenomenon is, no doubt, just another example of the "less is more" theory. In regard to time, we accomplish more when we hurry less. Simple as that—time just expands when we start to relax and slow down.

More importantly, something else happens as a result of stretching time as we refuse to be rushed. We begin to notice things we never had time to see before, or we see things we previously overlooked. We begin to experience things that are outside of our previously normal daily routine, things that are out of the ordinary, that are unusual, unique and special. As a result of slowing down, we discover this new-found time, and it can make our daily life a great deal more interesting and adventurous than it ever was before. We start to have the time of our lives, literally as well as figuratively.

Practice: *Creating More Time*

— If you are someone who's compulsively on time or early to everything (as I am), it can be an adventure to force yourself to be late now and then. Use the extra time for something fun.

— Whenever possible, find one thing to do during the day that you can do exclusively by itself from start to finish. Doing one small thing at a time to completion is actually an adventure in itself and provides a big burst of satisfaction during the day. Give it a try.

Spread Out

Most of us routinely try to go from point A to point B in the shortest distance possible. Almost habitually, we become so focused on taking the fastest, most direct route to where we are going that we can't think of anything else. That leaves little room for adventure throughout our day.

The solution to this linear life of over-efficiency is to start intentionally going out of our way once in a while. We can begin by purposefully taking the most interesting route (even if it's the long way) to our destination in order to simply see what there is to see along the way. The idea is to spread out and start moving in larger circles, literally, in order to explore more of the territory around us. It doesn't have to be a big deal. Even the smallest effort to break the linear patterns we've learned to live with and expand the space in which daily life takes place will make our lives more adventurous and exciting.

Practice: Taking a Different Path

— When possible, instead of taking the free-way, take surface streets through several of the neighborhoods on the way to your destination. I find it an adventure noticing what people do to their yards and houses in order to improve (they think) their appearance. Noticing the differences in homes and neighborhoods can tell us much about how our own life adventure compares with others'.

— The next time you're at a shopping center, instead of only looking for what you want, take time to just wander around awhile. Check out what people look like, how they dress and whatever else you can discern about them. Shopping centers and malls are, for many of us, our village, our town-gathering place, our community. Who we are is in part shaped by where we live and the people around us. I find it an adventure to visit, as it were, the place where I live.

There is no reason why we can't enjoy a life of daily adventure. We simply need to change a few old ideas to become increasingly and intentionally spontaneous to what life has to offer right now.

About This Chapter

Here are six suggestions or six action steps or six questions to help transform the ideas in this chapter into A **Really Radical Spiritually Adventurous Life**. Write your responses on these pages just as if this were a workbook or on a separate sheet of paper (if you prefer privacy, may want to loan the book to someone, etc.).

1. What caught your attention or was of particular interest to you in this chapter?

2. Any new ideas or possible adventures you might want to think about after reading this chapter?

3. What have you not thought about that this chapter has brought to your attention?

4. What would be one small step you could do in the next 24 hours to experiment with this chapter?

5. How might you sabotage or resist experimenting, with baby steps, for more adventure in your life (look for information, in this book, that can help to release resistance with _The Ten Step Miracle_ or _Bio-spiritual Focusing_)?

6. What type of additional support might you need to help transform daily life into an amazingly adventurous life? Like- minded friends, groups, a mentor or sponsor? Your own "inner allies" (as explained in this book) or listening to a "Higher Wisdom" by various means?

Make a quick list if you like.

**Further Notes, Thoughts
Or Ideas**

"It is a great art to saunter."

— *Henry David Thoreau*

CHAPTER **2**

Solo Adventures —

Wandering and Wondering On Your Own

There is something we can give ourselves that no one else can give us—we can give ourselves OUR SELF. One of the most practical and effective ways we can do this is to periodically set aside time for personal, solo, re-creational adventure. Taking time out solely for this purpose gives us the clear awareness of having a life of our own. Without this kind of awareness, we can't really share our lives with others, for we can't give what we don't have.

Time For Ourselves...
Not Time Alone

Taking time for ourselves, however, is not about being by ourselves. It is about being WITH ourselves. Taking time for ourselves is not about being alone; it is not about isolation. It is about the adventure we experience in continually discovering and un-covering the life within us while we are exploring life around us.

Solo adventures can come in many forms, ev-erything from going to the movies for a few hours to taking several days or more for a personal vaca-tion. Several types of solo adventures are the sub-ject of other chapters in this book.

Benefits of "Me Time"

Three things happen when we take time for per-sonal adventures of one kind or another.

Love Multiplies

The time we give to ourselves for personal en-joyment and satisfaction is a tangible and prac-tical form of self-love. It is self-love in action. It is an affirmation to our very soul that we are important and valuable. Some part of us deep within understands that we are lovable and that we are capable of loving ourselves exactly as we are. Some part of us deep within understands that, because we are spending quality time with ourselves, we are not entirely dependent upon outside approval and validation in order to feel loved. The time we give ourselves for solo ad-ventures gives us, in return, a more loving and lovable self. As a by-product of this form of self-love, we are better able to love someone else because we have more love to share. That's just how it works.

Stress Lessens

Another thing that happens when we are engaged in a personal adventure is that we experience a dramatic reduction in the amount of stress we may have been carrying around in our minds and bodies. It simply happens automatically. We don't have to do anything but enjoy being wherever we are, doing whatever we're doing. The stress becomes less intense all by itself. It's really amazing. I've found nothing works as well or as effectively.

Answers Arrive

Finally—and perhaps the most surprising thing of all—is that often in the course of actively pursuing our solo adventures, solutions will surface to some of the difficulties or problems we may have been unsuccessful at resolving in the past. It's as if the activity of the adventure in which we are engaged somehow cleanses our mind or rearranges the clutter in our brain so that there is room for new ideas or insights to appear. Answers to some of my most troubling questions have frequently been provided during the course of my solo adventures. It's quite incredible. I consider this benefit of taking time for self-adventures as nothing short of a miracle.

Do not fail to give yourself this wonderful gift that no one else can give you. It is not being selfish or self-centered. In fact, it is in many ways just the opposite. We owe it as much to those we love, as we do to ourselves, to take time to replenish and rejuvenate all the parts of us we want to share with others. Solo adventuring is one great way of re-creating the best of who we are.

Practice: Going Solo

— List four or five activities, events or places to visit that you would consider as potential solo adventure experiences.

— Rank this list according to how often you might like to experience each of them (for example, only once, once a month, every few months, once a year, etc.)

— Rank this list again according to convenience, such as: can do anytime, must plan ahead, will require significant preplanning, etc.

— Now rank again according to financial considerations—from easily affordable to must budget carefully to do.

— With all this information in mind, schedule in your appointment book which solo adventures you will do in the next six months or more.

About This Chapter

*Here are six suggestions or six action steps or six questions to help transform the ideas in this chapter into A **Really Radical Spiritually Adventurous Life**. Write your responses on these pages just as if this were a workbook or on a separate sheet of paper (if you prefer privacy, may want to loan the book to someone, etc.).*

1. What caught your attention or was of particular interest to you in this chapter?

2. Any new ideas or possible adventures you might want to think about after reading this chapter?

3. What have you not thought about that this chapter has brought to your attention?

4. What would be one small step you could do in the next 24 hours to experiment with this chapter?

5. How might you sabotage or resist experimenting, with baby steps, for more adventure in your life (look for information, in this book, that can help to release resistance with <u>The Ten Step Miracle</u> or <u>Bio-spiritual Focusing</u>)?

6. What type of additional support might you need to help transform daily life into an amazingly adventurous life? Like- minded friends, groups, a mentor or sponsor? Your own "inner allies" (as explained in this book) or listening to a "Higher wisdom" by various means?

Make a quick list if you like.

**Further Notes, Thoughts
Or Ideas**

"If you can't find harmony and spiritual dimensions in ordinary life, they are no where to be found."

— *Mark Juergensmeyer*

CHAPTER **3**

At Home Adventures —
A Slice of Heaven In Our Backyard

How often do we think about traveling around the world and exploring far-off places? That would certainly be an adventure. A longing to visit new and exciting places is very common. Rarely does anyone think about the adventure of exploring in their own backyard. That mundane, boring place—adventurous? Yes, right under your nose, where you live, can be a curious, fascinating place for an adventure.

Our homes, our backyards and our neighborhoods hold a promise of wondrous delights appealing to our senses of sight, sound, smell and touch. Give it a try. Take some time to simply visit a specific part of the property outside your living space and allow yourself to be fully present to your immediate surroundings. Pay attention to all the sounds. Do you hear birds singing or wind rustling in the trees? Pay attention to the colors, the green and red hues in the plant life. Pick up and touch several natural objects—rocks or plants. Feel their texture. Take a deep breath, enjoying the air in your body. Smell the air. Be aware of your entire body's experience—sight, smell, sound and touch.

It can even be an adventure to walk slowly through your home, visiting each room. Notice each room's personal environment. What curious notions come to you? What things have you noticed before and haven't looked at for a long time? Maybe you will see things for which you feel grateful. Maybe you will want to change the environment to better suit your senses. You can make visiting your own home a truly new adventure.

Our bodies and our minds need these types of brief, frequent adventures. They are mini-vacations for our concerns and difficulties. These little "living in the moment" adventures can be a great source of happiness just when we need it the most.

By being attentive to all your physical senses, you will be fulfilling a deep hunger to feel more alive and to satisfy the longing for a more adventurous everyday life. This is as important to your life as eating and sleeping. You are feeding your soul, your spirit for adventure.

Adventuring in your own immediate environment is cheap. The only price is taking the time to wander and wonder and to pay attention.

Practice: The Joy of Exploring

   — Take ten minutes to notice what is curious, unique, special or fascinating while slowly wandering around:

    (A) Your backyard or common area where you live

    (B) Your home

    (C) Your neighborhood or general vicinity

If your mind wanders to unsettling thoughts, just gently bring yourself back to the moment.

   — Find three things for which you're grateful in your surroundings.

   — Notice what you would want to change—if anything.

About This Chapter

Here are six suggestions or six action steps or six questions to help transform the ideas in this chapter into A **Really Radical Spiritually Adventurous Life**. *Write your responses on these pages just as if this were a workbook or on a separate sheet of paper (if you prefer privacy, may want to loan the book to someone, etc.).*

1. What caught your attention or was of particular interest to you in this chapter?

2. Any new ideas or possible adventures you might want to think about after reading this chapter?

3. What have you not thought about that this chapter has brought to your attention?
4. What would be one small step you could do in the next 24 hours to experiment with this chapter?

5. How might you sabotage or resist experimenting, with baby steps, for more adventure in your life (look for information, in this book, that can help to release resistance with <u>The Ten Step Miracle</u> or <u>Bio-spiritual Focusing</u>)?

6. What type of additional support might you need to help transform daily life into an amazingly adventurous life? Like- minded friends, groups, a mentor or sponsor? Your own "inner allies" (as explained in this book) or listening to a "Higher Wisdom" by various means?

Make a quick list if you like.

**Further Notes, Thoughts
Or Ideas**

"Variety is the spice of life that gives it all its flavour."

– William Cowper

CHAPTER 4

Connecting With Our Kids:
Adventures With
Fun and Feelings

Aaron, my fifteen-year old, comes home from school. He and I jump in the car for our special time together. He asks, "What do you want to do?"

"I don't know," I respond, "I've got to think. We have two hours before we must get back for dinner with Mom and your sisters."

Together we start brainstorming all the possibilities: play catch, get a video, play gin rummy or chess, or ride bikes. Eventually we decide to play catch and then go to the batting cages and arcade games. During this time we talk and share feelings and have fun. We connect. The adventure becomes a backdrop for caring attention.

Planning these little adventures or festive expeditions with our children and giving them time, as an expression of love, is the greatest gift we can give them. Our children view this quality time together as: "I'm loved, special, important, worthy of time and attention" versus "I'm less than, not worth the time, or my parents' work is more important."

Making this adventure time happen is not easy, but you can do it even with a busy schedule. I have three children ages 15, 12 and 10. I love them dearly. Love demands caring attention. Love demands action, not just empty promises of "maybe later or someday…"

Six Practical Steps
For Adventuring With Your Children

1. First, put your own house in order. Take care of yourself so you are not resentful of the time you spend with your children. Taking time for fun and relaxation with yourself, your partner or your friends is self-care. It is not selfishness. Without self-nurturing, you cannot give to your children. You cannot give on an empty tank. When you are full and replenished, or at least in the process of self-care, you're more mindful and attentive to planning and sharing with your children. Create a self-care plan of five to ten simple, enjoyable, self-nurturing activities and try a different one each week.

2. After replenishing your own tank, start with small chunks of time for adventures with your children, maybe an hour to three hours maximum. Think about how you can create a space in your busy calendar where you know you will be present emotionally and physically. Avoid distractions such

as a cellular phone, beepers or other work items. Surrender to this time. Clearly see this time as a priority. Slowly ease into it. Experiment with times during the week with each child. Then write this time in your calendar and make it just as important as any date—if not *the* most important one. Calendaring translates into commitment.

3. <u>Find fun adventures that you too will enjoy with your children</u>. Brainstorm all the possibilities before you decide. You never know when a great idea will pop up spontaneously. Do not stop and evaluate the pros and cons as you think of each idea. You might squelch the creative process of idea inventing. Talk about all the possibilities: a garage sale adventure, a visit to the park, a ball game, a trip to the bookstore. Take care to think and input ideas that will allow close moments of sharing and talking. You'll be amazed at how the activity is often less important than being there and just listening, sharing, feeling, validating, and empathizing. These are all ways of saying, "I love you, I care about you, my wonderful, precious child."

4. <u>Decide on the adventure</u>. Take all of your ideas and come up with a win-win agreement where both of your needs are met. For example, both of you may feel a need to get physical through playing catch or shooting some hoops. If negotiations fail to come up with a common activity, then you can do a trade-off or split the time into two small activities, one for each of you, or the one this week is your choice and next week the choice is mine.

Therefore you can cooperate on a win-win agreement or compromise and do a trade-off.

Also, as long as you're not resentful, you can compromise if you still cannot agree on an adventure. You can plan to be totally spontaneous and decide in the moment—just drive in the car and see what comes. Just let the desire in the moment dictate what you will do: "Oh, there's a bookstore, do you want to go there?" The process of brainstorming and agreeing ensures that you are both listening and caring for each other. Without this kind of sharing, you could end up feeling resentful and obligated about the time you're spending with your children. This process of decision-making teaches your children relationship skills, a huge benefit of adventuring.

5. <u>Keep your promises</u>. What if an emergency or an unexpected event comes up which prevents your planned special time? Then, it is essential that you reschedule (on your calendar) a specific date or a window of time that you follow-up with your child. Make sure no promises are un-kept. Keep your agreements even if you have to postpone. Without this follow-up, the bond of love and trust will slowly deteriorate. If you find you are continually postponing these adventures because of work or other activities, find a way to rebalance your life that allows for special time with your children. Come to grips with any fear that sabotages this balance and try to overcome it. You may need help and support from your friends, clergy or a

counselor. Build the trust and love that creates healthy children.

6. <u>Move towards advanced adventuring with children</u>. As you progress from having regular weekly adventure time (with backup dates for interruptions), you can also plan special days or weekends or week-long adventure trips. Some of your bigger adventures can be cheap thrills. Budget adventuring is definitely possible by stating your money limits in advance while planning. You can even prepare lists of ideas of things to do with little or no money. The bottom line is that these festive expeditions provide a common shared experience for giving and receiving and providing love and attention. The activity itself is less important than actually being together. The activities are just vehicles to be mindful of your child in the moment, to listen, to pay attention and to be there for your child. Often unexpected shared feelings and intimacies bubble up and add further closeness with your youngsters.

Special adventures are, of course, not the only time you spend with your children. All of these special adventures, big or small, are part of the whole texture of time spent with the younger members of the family, including the more mundane and necessary activities associated with school projects, homework and chores. However, when you add the element of focused special attention, you have given and received the greatest gift you and your children can ever have—the gift of the Precious Present.

About This Chapter

*Here are six suggestions or six action steps or six questions to help transform the ideas in this chapter into A **Really Radical Spiritually Adventurous Life**. Write your responses on these pages just as if this were a workbook or on a separate sheet of paper (if you prefer privacy, may want to loan the book to someone, etc.).*

1. What caught your attention or was of particular interest to you in this chapter?

2. Any new ideas or possible adventures you might want to think about after reading this chapter?

3. What have you not thought about that this chapter has brought to your attention?

4. What would be one small step you could do in the next 24 hours to experiment with this chapter?

5. How might you sabotage or resist experimenting, with baby steps, for more adventure in your life (look for information, in this book, that can help to release resistance with _The Ten Step Miracle_ or _Bio-spiritual Focusing_)?

6. What type of additional support might you need to help transform daily life into an amazingly adventurous life? Like- minded friends, groups, a mentor or sponsor? Your own "inner allies" (as explained in this book) or listening to a "Higher Wisdom" by various means?

Make a quick list if you like.

Further Notes, Thoughts Or Ideas

"The real voyage of discovery consists not in seeking new landscapes, but in having new eyes."

— *Marcel Proust*

CHAPTER 5

Vacation Travel Adventures –

Wherever I Go, There I Am, I Always Take Me With Me

Do you want a heavenly vacation or a vacation from hell? Do you want your vacations or getaways to bring you peace, renewal, joy and relaxation? Or do you want to be tension-filled, hurried and harried, trying to see and do everything while enjoying little, all the while fighting and hassling with your family or travel-mates or the travel personnel helping you?

Whether you choose short or long getaways, both provide opportunities for adventure, renewal, and relaxation. By getting away from your regular routine and being immersed with new stimuli, you can be challenged to enjoy the moment and go with the flow. But this was not my story in my early years, when I experienced the five basic false expectations of a vacation.

- The first false expectation is that the vacation will make me happy and that by going somewhere else, it will be better—where I am is not as good. I'm struggling here: over *there* is better. Over *there* is peace and paradise. I would go on vacations to feel better, not appreciating where I lived.

- The second false expectation is that I'm only okay if I bring work with me. I felt guilty if I didn't use the time to produce creatively. While on a trip to Mexico one year, I brought 20 books to read and study. This comforted my guilt of just relaxing and being.

- The third false expectation is that all interactions had to go perfectly well between my traveling mates and me. I created a huge, perfect, romantic picture of how the trip would go. Before I took my wife to Hawaii one year, I had overworked months prior and was very stressed out. My expectations for a perfect wonderful vacation were spoiled when we had a huge argument. We had no tools to work this through or to see the potential gift in the conflict. We managed to work through our difficulty, but we had wasted precious vacation time and had not learned from our experience.

- The fourth false expectation is that everything must go perfectly well on the trip. Any glitches or experiences with rude people will ruin the vacation. I remember a time on an airplane when I was very tired, having had only three hours of sleep. A steward was rude to me, and I began yelling at him. Fortunately, I apologized later for my part of the interaction.

- Finally, the fifth false expectation is that you must try to do everything on your vacation. I remember running all over London in my student years, hurried and harried and exhausted having seen everything from the Tower to St. Paul's Cathedral, but enjoying nothing. It was all a blur, but I had seen it, by golly!

Finding Joy by Breaking Free

To counter these false expectations or beliefs—which only bring more suffering—we have to gradually, with forgiveness, learn to live more in the precious present. Much of this book is about adventuring in the now—the only moment we can enjoy. Happiness can only be enjoyed right now, through being grateful for what you have in your own backyard, treasuring your memories, and learning the gift in adventuring. All the adventures in the book can be applied to your getaway or a travel experience.

- To counter the first false expectation that your vacation will make you happy, use the tools in this book to enjoy the life you have now. If you see and live life in gratitude for what you have, your vacation is simply an enhancement, not an end-all or be-all. I live in paradise in my home. If I go to Hawaii or anywhere else, I'm simply experiencing a different kind of paradise—not better. This perspective of living in the now, enjoying each moment before, during and after the vacation, makes *life* a vacation. Instead of "vacating", I am learning to be present wherever I am. Vacations become "presentations", learning experiences of being joyful in the present moment. I want every day to be an adventure or mini-vacation in and of itself instead of a struggle where I am, waiting to be happy when the weekend or my vacation comes. This is the overall meaning of adventure in this book. The greatest calling is to live life as an adventure every moment, and be open to gifts in joyful events as well as in the grief or adverse ones, too.

- To counter the second false expectation of working or struggling while on vacation—do bring work if you want to. But bring your passion or hobby with you to enjoy as an adventure within an adventure. I am an actor in community theater. I recently went to Hawaii and lovingly practiced my songs from old shows and lines and monologues for new ones. I used the expanse of time on the vacation to spontaneously have fun with my hobby.

- To counter the third false expectation of having to have a perfect, romantic getaway—make your trip an extension of the romance you are already cultivating at home. For example, my wife and I have never stopped dating. Almost every Saturday night for 26 years of married life we have had a date. Besides cherishing small things through the week, we also give one special gift or loving behavior to each other each week.

  Again, the vacation is an enhancement of what we are doing at home. If there is an argument at home or on vacation, we use the tools of time-outs and couples dialogue to learn from our difficulties just as we would at home. Great gifts have come out of some of our arguments. Conflict is inevitable between people who love one another. We can use these conflicts wherever we are, to grow and learn.

- To counter the fourth false expectation that no glitches should happen on your vacation—well, we will really suffer with this expectation. On a family trip to Hawaii in 1990 with my wife and three young children, we went to the rental car office, obtained our station wagon and drove to our expected beautiful hotel overlooking the beach. The only problem was the hotel was gone. It had been blown away the year before during Hurricane Iniki. Our travel company had reserved us in a hotel on a bluff which no longer existed. I'll never forget looking over the bluff in shock and amazement.

An old man came out of a building next to the empty lot we faced. Upon hearing about our phantom hotel, he invited us into his condo. Then he told us how he had survived the hurricane. He asked us to stay with him. We declined his kind gesture—but his story and invitation remain a gift to me and my family. Later we found a better place to stay than the original hotel. We used the glitch as a gift; we made lemonade from lemons.

- Finally, to counter the fifth false expectation of trying to do everything on your vacation—learn to slow down and enjoy each moment; learning to wander and wonder will greatly enhance your vacation. Practice this at home in your own backyard before you go. Connect to nature on your trip. Anything that is real—not man-made—for at least some of the time will keep you grounded in the here and now. Going to a park, sitting on a bench, watching the sunset can be more wonderful than all the hot spots that the travel guides tell you about.

Also, leave something for your next trip. Purposefully do not do everything so you'll enjoy coming back to something. I had been to Italy twice before I finally went to Venice. By holding back on Venice over the years, I kept the mystery and intrigue of this beautiful place intact. On my third visit, I made the trip to Venice with my youngest daughter. What a beautiful place. I discovered other places in Italy where I have not traveled so I'll be intrigued to someday return.

By slowing down and wandering and wondering and not having to do it all, you actually will deepen your enjoyment. Unexpected gifts will come to you when you are open to them—not just the "must do's" travel brochures tell you about. I have found many hidden beaches and interesting stores and parks by simply wandering about. I have met many beautiful people when I decided to slow down and relax and reach out in conversation.

So the theme is to adventure, go slow, go with the flow, to enjoy each moment. If you get stuck in one of the five false expectations, that's okay. Forgive yourself and learn from them. Every day can be a miracle, an adventure—and a vacation.

About This Chapter

*Here are six suggestions or six action steps or six questions to help transform the ideas in this chapter into A **Really Radical Spiritually Adventurous Life**. Write your responses on these pages just as if this were a workbook or on a separate sheet of paper (if you prefer privacy, may want to loan the book to someone, etc.).*

1. What caught your attention or was of particular interest to you in this chapter?

2. Any new ideas or possible adventures you might want to think about after reading this chapter?

3. What have you not thought about that this chapter has brought to your attention?

4. What would be one small step you could do in the next 24 hours to experiment with this chapter?

5. How might you sabotage or resist experimenting, with baby steps, for more adventure in your life (look for information, in this book, that can help to release resistance with _The Ten Step Miracle_ or _Bio-spiritual Focusing_)?

6. What type of additional support might you need to help transform daily life into an amazingly adventurous life? Like- minded friends, groups, a mentor or sponsor? Your own "inner allies" (as explained in this book) or listening to a "Higher wisdom" by various means?

Make a quick list if you like.

**Further Notes, Thoughts
Or Ideas**

"Nine times out of ten, when you extend your arms to someone, they will step in, because basically they need precisely what you need."

— *Leo Buscaglia*

CHAPTER 6

Adventures of Intimate Relationships –
And Traversing Marriage Mountains

The adventure of being in a close relationship can surely bring more love and intimacy into our lives. Often that love and intimacy grows out of conflicts and thus the process of learning how to resolve them. In fact, conflict is inevitable in any relationship and can paradoxically become an adventure towards creating greater love, closeness and even freedom.

One couple we will call John and Mary had a pattern of having verbal fights over money issues. John loved to save every dime that he and Mary earned, in an effort to plan toward a secure retirement. John was serious and responsible, always planning ahead. Mary was just the opposite. She enjoyed spending whatever she earned. Mary was a very spontaneous person, a bit overindulgent, but certainly fun-loving. John and Mary, like many of us, married their opposite.

At first this difference was a real thrill. John enjoyed Mary's enthusiasm for living. It influenced him to open up his own suppressed joy. Mary loved John's sensible consistency. This trait encouraged her to balance her immediate need for fun with more long-range preparation and goal setting. Both partners in the beginning complemented each other. Each partner was a teacher to the other. After a while, though, this infatuation period ended, and a deep power struggle ensued. Unconscious fears surfaced as John and Mary tried to control and change each other.

Their opposite natures started to clash. The very thing that they liked about each other initially became the thing they most disliked. Huge verbal fights ensued with criticism and contempt on John's part while Mary became defensive, withdrew in silence and became depressed. Their marriage was drifting toward divorce.

Mary decided on one last effort. She purchased several books designed to help couples resolve conflicts. She persuaded John to read them, and in addition, go to couple's counseling and attend related workshops. Instead of sinking into the deep hole of blame, John and Mary used this adversity to reconnect. A great adventure resulted as both were willing to learn how to resolve this and other conflicts in their relationship. The seven steps they learned from their counseling moved them towards more closeness and love in their relationship.

The Seven Steps to Resolving Conflicts
Step One: <u>Becoming responsible for own part of problem</u>

John and Mary were willing to become accountable for their own negative fighting behavior. John took responsibility for his self-defeating behavior of name-calling and criticism. Mary saw her stone-walling treatment as protection, but not helpful in standing up for herself. Both learned to become assertive rather than passive or aggressive.

Step Two: <u>Creating a common vision</u>

With help, they created a balanced vision of saving for retirement and having fun in the present. They wrote a mission statement. They realized both of them wanted a balanced future.

Step Three: <u>Going inside</u>

John and Mary listened to the false assumptions and unmet needs underneath their self-defeating behavior. John realized he was afraid of appearing weak if he couldn't control the money. He had learned a false belief from his father—that money equals power and without it he was nothing. He began to realize that money indeed could give him the power of choice, but it was only energy, a token in exchange for the time spent earning it. He learned to feel okay with or without money. Mary likewise learned to have fun with or without money. She let go of a belief that money equals freedom and fun. She thought she had to have and spend money to get pleasure. She learned to let go of her fear and false belief and still have a good time.

Over time, both John and Mary released deeply imbedded false beliefs that they were holding unconsciously. This was causing their power struggle. This inner adventure of healing released much pain and suffering. They learned to use many techniques such as Focusing, Hypnotherapy and Sentence Completion to release old false assumptions.

Step Four: <u>Taking Time-outs</u>

Occasionally John and Mary will slip into old habits, especially if they are <u>H</u>ungry, <u>A</u>ngry, <u>L</u>onely or <u>T</u>ired. They have learned to HALT and take time-outs and to continue to own and release these beliefs over time.

No one ever reaches perfection. This adventure is about improvement. Taking time-outs when old issues come up is natural and to be expected. During time-outs of 10 minutes, 1 hour, or 24 hours, each partner can go inside and become accountable. They can then own their part, forgive themselves and their partner, and regroup for a discussion.

Step Five: <u>Developing a Couples Council</u>

John and Mary then created a regular time, a couple's council, to revisit their mission statement and money issues or other problems in their relationship.

The couple's council provided a safe time each week to plan and set goals for fun and savings. The vision of balance requires an action plan—specific steps for calendaring and follow through.

Step Six: <u>Creating Safe Dialogue</u>
John and Mary learned how to discuss their differences through a process called Couples Sharing. With this tool, each person repeats back what is heard from the other and gives empathy (not agreement) to the other. By listening this way, new ideas often emerge automatically to resolve an impasse. This is a continual process of transforming conflict into growth.

Step Seven: <u>Seeking Support</u>
Finally, John and Mary continued to commit to their growth by participating in a monthly couples support group called Marriage Encounter. They also committed to attend one workshop for couples each year. These groups provide an opportunity to meet like-minded couples who share their same commitment to making love an adventure—an adventure that requires work and needs support. They realize that their relationship is worth the effort.

<u>Epilogue</u>
While many of their neighbors have separated or just live in misery, John and Mary are not settling for a spiritual divorce. They continue to work at love. They realize that their relationship is worth the effort

that love requires and that love is not only a feeling and caring. The adventure of love is primarily an action of becoming accountable, self-loving, going inside, releasing false beliefs and creating an ongoing structure of forgiveness and tools to maintain this love. Love means having a safe structure to meet and discuss along with having the outer support of like-minded couples.

Practice: Nurturing Your Relationship
1. Visioning
Sit down separately first and write down your dreams and visions (not specific goals) for your relationship. Then sit down together and combine your separate dreams into a common wish or dream list. Put down only those you agree upon in principle. Let go of specific outcomes and goal setting until later.

2. Taking Time-outs
Practice taking time-outs before you really need to. It will be easier to do in a real conflict if you have done several "fake time-outs" with each other beforehand
Easy Two Step Time-Out Process
(a.) Both partners agree in advance that either partner (without getting permission from the other) can call a time-out. One partner says: "I need a time-out. I'll be back in __ minutes"
The other has to go along—no veto power. Both partners separate physically during time-outs. The partner calling the time-out has to

come back at the time stated. The time must be specific—not, "I'll talk to you later." Couples may want to pre-arrange a 20 minute come-back time unless it's too late at night. If it is very late, then at the earliest next connection time—either morning or evening the following day would be appropriate. Do several fake time-outs over the next week where you practice using the words above. The only difference is you insert, "I'm taking a fake time-out. I'll be back in 20 minutes." You do not have to leave as you practice this tool—you are developing a new habit or ritual.

(b.) Explore your hidden assumptions when you're upset with your partner, especially during a time-out. Underlying most arguments are false assumptions or misinterpretations. Remember, we are rarely upset for what we really think we are upset about. You may be fighting about sex or money, but hidden assumptions are often the real reason for conflict.

3. The Ten Minute Miracle

During a time-out period, or any time, do The Ten Minute Miracle as described in chapter 12. Intuitive wisdom can come to you to help resolve issues.

About This Chapter

Here are six suggestions or six action steps or six questions to help transform the ideas in this chapter into A **Really Radical Spiritually Adventurous Life**. *Write your responses on these pages just as if this were a workbook or on a separate sheet of paper (if you prefer privacy, may want to loan the book to someone, etc.).*

1. What caught your attention or was of particular interest to you in this chapter?

2. Any new ideas or possible adventures you might want to think about after reading this chapter?

3. What have you not thought about that this chapter has brought to your attention?

4. What would be one small step you could do in the next 24 hours to experiment with this chapter?

5. How might you sabotage or resist experimenting, with baby steps, for more adventure in your life (look for information, in this book, that can help to release resistance with _The Ten Step Miracle_ or _Bio-spiritual Focusing_)?

6. What type of additional support might you need to help transform daily life into an amazingly adventurous life? Like- minded friends, groups, a mentor or sponsor? Your own "inner allies" (as explained in this book) or listening to a "Higher wisdom" by various means?

Make a quick list if you like.

**Further Notes, Thoughts
Or Ideas**

"He who has health has hope;
He who has hope has
everything."

— Arabic Proverb

CHAPTER 7

Adventures for Living Well and Being Well

Looking Good And Feeling Fine

Learning to take better care of our bodies has become a matter of incredible interest in recent years. Never before has so much attention been focused on how to slow down the aging process and maintain the highest physical level of functioning possible.

Only recently have terms like "free radicals" become household words. That term sounds like it belongs more in political circles than in health circles. This one idea alone (that we can slow down the rate of free radical damage to our cells) has awakened many of us to exploring new ways of taking better care of our bodies.

Living longer and living better is a real possibility. Adding years to our life and life to our years can certainly be a worthwhile endeavor. There are those who believe that we may soon be able to live well past 100 years of age. Some even think that if the rate of new understanding about the aging process continues at the pace now under way, we may some day be able to live indefinitely. Now *that* would be the ultimate adventure!

Aging and Free Radicals

Why do we age? Many theories exist to answer this question. The famed Swedish studies of 10,000 pairs of twins showed that longevity has mainly to do with lifestyle and much less to do with genetics. This means we have the opportunity to influence our quality of life and more than "make do" with what we inherited.

Of the approximately 300 modern theories of aging presently espoused in scientific literature, the most accepted explanation of why we age is the increase of free radicals in our bodies. In 1956, Deham Harmon, M.D. discovered that highly-charged atoms—molecules or compounds that are missing electrons—wreak havoc on our systems, carrying cancer and other diseases. Free radicals are the culprit. They come from our environment, our own bodies' oxidation of food to energy, smoking, various toxins, and even medications. Free radicals from these sources sweep to the cells' DNA, fatty acids and proteins, and swipe electrons; this prevents the cells from functioning properly. The taking of an electron creates imbalances because the electron needs to be paired for balance.

For example, if you spend too much time in sunlight, the ultraviolet light will knock off an electron from a molecule in your skin. The affected molecule swipes an electron from a neighboring molecule, setting off a chain reaction and havoc in the body. Skin cancer could be the result.

Free radicals—the primary cause of aging—are also multiplied when there is a lack of healthy food and exercise. Fortunately, the body itself helps stop free radicals by generating antioxidants, using each cell's own internal defense mechanisms. But as we age, this system becomes less effective. We need to eat foods and take supplements rich in antioxidants, as well as exercise regularly to reduce free radicals and aid in longevity.

Fighting Free Radicals With Diet

In Dr. Art Hister's thought-provoking book, *Dr. Art Hister's Guide to Living a Long & Healthy Life*, he recommends a Mediterranean type diet to increase antioxidants and decrease free radicals. Some of the guidelines include:

1) Eat 8 servings per day of fruits and vegetables rich in antioxidants.
2) Eat unsaturated fats (30% of your daily intake), from nuts, avocados, olives and fish.
3) Eat beans and whole grain foods.
4) Consume a modest amount of red wine.

I would suggest that if you don't like wine with your meals, then drink grape juice. It has as many antioxidants as wine without the alcohol.

The Mediterranean diet has abundant antioxidants, reduces bad cholesterol LDL (low density lipoprotein) and lowers blood pressure. It also helps to reduce abdominal fat and increase insulin levels, and assists in better arterial functioning. It lowers the risk of cancer, diabetes, Alzheimer's disease, stroke and arthritis. Other dieticians and nutritionists recommend un-canned foods in season with intense color. Brightly-colored foods contain a variety of vitamins and minerals and photo chemicals. Use oils rich in Omega-3, such as olive, canola, sesame or walnut. Obtain your protein from fish, poultry, eggs, soft cheeses and lean meats, or vegetable sources such as legumes or green vegetables.

Along with this diet, Dr. Hister (and many other health experts) recommends:

1) Eat less at each meal—half of the normal portions.

2) Slow down and enjoy each bite.

3) Eat a hearty and healthy breakfast, less at lunch, and even less at dinner—or like a king at breakfast, a queen at lunch, and a pauper at night.

4) Avoid fad diets like Atkins and the Zone, because of the lack of documented long-term effects. Having a balanced diet of 40% protein, 30% carbs and 30% fats is best.

5) Watch portion size—how much you eat and calories of what you eat. Calories *do* count.

6) Avoid foods with hydrogenated or partially hydrogenated fats. Look at the food label on the product. Foods with these unhealthy chemicals are often spreads, snacks, baked goods and fried foods.

7) Eat only when you are hungry. Avoid eating to comfort your stress or numb your emotions. Know when you are full. Stop eating when you feel these sensations. Get in touch with your sensations. Get in touch with your unique body sensations of feeling full.

8) Eat sitting and not while watching television or reading. Pay attention to your body and how much you eat without distractions.

9) Taking a daily vitamin is advised to supplement any nutrients we may miss in our daily food plan.

10) Consider a formal nutrition program (i.e. Weight Watchers' point system)

Move It!
Exercising Your Right to
Good Health

Ultimately, eating a healthy diet is not enough to ensure improvement in overall health. Consumer Reports surveyed 32,000 dieters who had reached a normal weight and kept it off for over a year. The number one factor in ongoing weight loss was exercise.

An American study of 3,000 successful weight losers (66 pounds average weight loss maintained for at least 5 ½ years) also showed that exercise was the key factor. In fact, the kind of nutrition plan or diet was secondary and less significant. Exercise was the primary reason for successful, sustained results.

Exercise significantly reduces heart disease, cancer, diabetes, erectile dysfunction and memory loss. It helps promote a healthy immune system, looser joints, good sleep patterns, as well as decreases lower back pain. Exercise allows you to eat more, and to maintain independence as you age.

The kind of exercise we need consists of three types:

1) Stretching
2) Aerobic—activity that increases the heart rate
3) Anaerobic or resistance training with light weights, or push-ups or sit-ups (appropriate to your age)

Always consult your doctor before embarking on any exercise program to determine special needs and pacing based on your current health condition.

Here are some specific ideas on embarking on an exercise program.

1) Start small—take "baby steps". Don't over-do it.

2) Alternate each day with different exercises to allow muscles and tendons to rest.

3) Pick exercises you enjoy doing—something that will allow you to break a sweat or perspire and raise your heart rate for aerobic purposes. You can purchase a heart rate monitor to assist you keep track of your effort.

4) Brisk walking 30 minutes a day, 5-6 days a week, will lower your heart attack risk by 25% according to a leading study. But any exercise that raises your heart rate while not jarring your joints and tendons will do: vigorous dancing, swimming, and biking are just a few ideas.

5) Buddy up or join a health club to get support from others. Hire a trainer as outside support. Or exercise alone, like I do. I alternate brisk walking and riding my mountain bike. I love it. I am outdoors, breathing fresh air and enjoying nature at the same time.

6) Make exercise a priority—write down all the benefits to motivate you to sustain you in your long-term plan. Most people last two or three weeks, get bored, overdo it, or get injured and stop.

7) Get good equipment at your local sports equipment store. To avoid injury, make sure they are high quality and fit you.

8) Drink lots of water—8 glasses a day.

9) Pick a time that suits your best chance of

following through.

10) Above all, be patient, enjoy yourself and evaluate your program. If you fall off, forgive yourself, find out why, and do something different, or find a different way of motivating yourself. You can always start again shortly after a misstep.

The Body Beautiful

There's a lot more we can do besides exercise and supplementing our diet to aid our bodies in looking better longer and being physically fit. This is where the real adventure begins.

Let's start with massage. While still popular, Swedish massage is just one of many different types of massage available today. Everything from healing touch massage to deep tissue work, from reflexology to Watsu (massage in water) to energy balancing massage, Reiki massage, polarity and Orthobionomy massage is designed to benefit us in specific ways.

Skin care treatment can be another facet of bio-physical adventure. Have you ever had a facial? It's a combination of massage and deep skin cleaning and moisturizing. There are also many new products being introduced all the time which can help rejuvenate the skin and soften wrinkles. Take some time to check out all the new skin care products on the market at your local drugstore or cosmetic counter of any large department store. That alone can be an adventure.

Many cosmetic sections of larger department stores offer women free makeup applications and consultations. Not only that, they frequently give free samples of many of their products.

Clothes are another aspect of bio-physical adventure. Often people think they must wear the clothes they own until they are worn out. If everyone did that, there would be no clothes to give to charity. The way we attire our bodies can have an impact on how others see us which, in turn, can impact how we think and feel about ourselves. Style is important. Styles change. Staying current with the times, in all areas of our lives, including the clothes we wear, is of value in living better, longer. Subscribing to a fashion magazine is not a guilty pleasure.

More Ways to Nurture Health

Besides the food plans and exercise ideas in this chapter, to enjoy a long, quality life, it is imperative to:

1. Stop smoking.
2. Learn tools to manage your emotions for stress relief.
3. Maintain a support system.
4. Develop a philosophy, spiritual or religious life that promotes unconditional self-love and love and forgiveness of others.

It goes without showing any detailed evidence that smoking is harmful to your health. Stop smoking any way you can. Use the patch, gum, non-smoking classes or support groups like Smokers Anonymous (nicanonymous). Stop cold turkey if you can. Studies show using two or more methods together are best, especially if one includes a support group. It is a myth that you will automatically gain weight if you stop smoking. You will, if you don't find alternative healthy ways of reducing stress. Emotional eating is the leading cause of overeating—eating when we are stressed-out instead of exercising, meditating, or other practices to manage emotions.

Learn to manage your emotions by developing an inner spiritual life based on compassion and love. Many of the adventures in this book will aid you in developing inner peace. This will reduce stress and help in living longer. Find a healing church or 12 Step recovery program, or a book club or join any club where you have fun and enjoy people. Find a cause to fight for with other people—a political party, or any passionate, purposeful group you like. All these will aid you, along with a healthy food plan and exercise.

Go forth and live longer with a healthy, fulfilling heart, body, mind and soul-tools this book provides.

About This Chapter

*Here are six suggestions or six action steps or six questions to help transform the ideas in this chapter into A **Really Radical Spiritually Adventurous Life**. Write your responses on these pages just as if this were a workbook or on a separate sheet of paper (if you prefer privacy, may want to loan the book to someone, etc.).*

1. What caught your attention or was of particular interest to you in this chapter?

2. Any new ideas or possible adventures you might want to think about after reading this chapter?

3. What have you not thought about that this chapter has brought to your attention?

4. What would be one small step you could do in the next 24 hours to experiment with this chapter?

5. How might you sabotage or resist experimenting, with baby steps, for more adventure in your life (look for information, in this book, that can help to release resistance with <u>The Ten Step Miracle</u> or <u>Bio-spiritual Focusing</u>)?

6. What type of additional support might you need to help transform daily life into an amazingly adventurous life? Like- minded friends, groups, a mentor or sponsor? Your own "inner allies" (as explained in this book) or listening to a "Higher wisdom" by various means?

Make a quick list if you like.

**Further Notes, Thoughts
Or Ideas**

"What lies behind us and what lies ahead of us are tiny matters compared to what lies within us."

– Ralph Waldo Emerson

CHAPTER **8**

Creating Greater Creativity
A Journey To Real Joy

Every human being has creative potential. Simply put, creativity is doing <u>what you love to do</u>. When you do what you love, you will experience more happiness, inner contentment, joy and vitality. Creativity is not just for the gifted few who are so talented and great. We *all* have gifts to share that will bring joy to ourselves and others, even if we don't rise to the level of "great artist" or "virtuoso"; creativity is often stifled by this major myth. Other myths are that we must spend all of our time at one creative endeavor, or we shouldn't do it unless we can make money at it. We are told skeptically, "You're very talented good, but don't give up your day job."

Learning to express yourself creatively can be an incredibly wonderful adventure. Expanding your creative potential is also good medicine for both the body and the mind. Through gardening, music, working with children, sports, or whatever you love, an inner pharmacy of chemicals (endorphins and serotonins) will support you. You'll receive a natural high, a gift from this inner chemistry. If you are not proactive in your life with creative purpose, you can become a reactive victim to life's trials and unfairness.

Finding Your Passion

What if you don't know what you love? What if you only love what is not good for you, like too many chocolate sundaes or pizzas or double martinis? You can learn to replace these escapes. You can learn to find and follow your passions and creativity.

To expand your creative potential, you need to begin with some basics. You'll need a backpack filled with tools to carry with you on this journey. You'll need a pen, notebook and a friend or two. A calendar will help. The most important basic tool is intangible—your willingness to experiment, to take small risks, and to make mistakes. The entire journey has six transitions:

1. <u>Preparation</u> of your backpack;

2. <u>Inspiration</u> or dreaming which direction you're going to go to find your heart's desire;

3. <u>Transformation</u>, in which the dream transforms your inner life and you release self-criticism and rigid logic to let your intuition guide you;

4. <u>Perspiration</u>—make the effort to take experimental action, evaluate small steps to see if they are helping or hindering your dream;

5. <u>Celebration</u> of the journey, which in fact, you want to be doing all along your journey;

6. <u>Rededication</u> to new journeys as you spiral upwards.

Preparation: Filling Your Backpack

Like preparing for any journey, making sure you have everything you need makes the trip more pleasant. Here are some practices to take with you.

<u>Flow writing</u>

Each morning or evening take time to write for 10 minutes about how you're feeling and what you need and want. Do this flow as a stream of consciousness writing as if you're babbling like a baby. Disregard punctuation, grammar and spelling. This exercise is for your eyes only. From this writing, you will slowly uncover what you might love and need for fulfillment. Needs are expressions of what you love. As an example, from daily flow writing, I discovered I needed more movement in my life. My body ached in the morning, but I attributed this to growing older. What came in the writing was a need to stretch more. Also, I adapted several yoga postures that I loved. Today I have no more chronic lower back problems, which had plagued me for years. Besides Flow Writing, you can use the Ten Minute Miracle (chapter 12) or Biospirtual Focusing (chapter 10).

Companionship

On your journey, find a friend or two or three for companionship. Having a kindred spirit with you makes the journey safer and more fun. Caring company can enhance your creativity. Your buddy, mentor or teacher needs to be encouraging and empathetic of your dreams and passions. However, beware of false guides, quick fixes, or gurus bearing messages like "You can go right to your bliss without any perspiration or frustration". Finding and following your passion is not just about thinking good thoughts and everything will be okay. Chanting "I'm okay, you're okay" is not enough. Neither does the quest for creativity have to be bleak, gloomy or lonely. It is a balance of feeling all your feelings—sad, mad, scared, and longing—which can lead to joy and contentment.

Inner Support Network

Develop a sense of inner support from a connection to a higher power or inner allies. This could be a belief and dialogue with a loving God of your understanding. Or, if you are an atheist or agnostic, you could practice any method to develop a sense of inner safety, to affirm your worth and validate your dreams. Native Americans used spirit guides in the form of animals or ancestors to support their life journey. The one common factor in civilizations throughout history is that all believed in something higher (more than the willful self-centered ego) to guide them internally. It didn't matter whether this was internal higher focus or an external higher power.

Challenge yourself to experiment with developing a sense of inner or outer support beyond the help of living humans. You will learn one of the greatest gifts—how to connect to your own inner authority for ideas, safety and love. Balance this inner support with healthy outer support from your buddies. Sometimes God has skin.

Commitment to Creativity
Make creativity a priority each day. Making creativity a priority in your daily life is the single most important item for preparation of your journey. Are you willing to pay the price for more peace, happiness and excitement in your life? Start small and set aside fifteen to thirty minutes a day. Reorder and let go of the activities that are less important to you.

Inspiration: Drawing a Map to Your Dreams
Now that you have made preparations for your journey (by packing the basics), you can begin brainstorming about what more you want to do.

Feed the Need
With your **flow writing or The Ten Minute Miracle or Biospiritual Focusing** as a vehicle, write down on separate pages any dreams or needs that bubble up from the writing. When you write in a stream of consciousness or babbling way, you

allow creative ideas and unmet needs to bubble up to your awareness. These intuitive knowings will help you satisfy your own longings. You won't fall into the trap of letting your vision be just trying to please someone else. So instead of learning to play the piano to get your family's approval, you'll be learning the piano for *you*, to express your love for this beautiful vehicle of expression. Your primary body feeling of contentment resonates within you, not from the outside. It's nice to get the affirmation from others, but it is not the primary motivation. It's the joy of the process of playing and learning itself, even with the frustrations and disappointments along the way.

As you continue to flow write, you may see a pattern of the same longings or wants and needs. For example, you hear "I need love and companionship" over and over again in your writing. Or you write that you want to travel for adventure and relaxation, a change of pace. If you get specific and come to changes like "I want to go to Hawaii" or "I hate my job", go underneath these wants to the specific unmet needs: "I want to travel to Hawaii for relaxation and adventure needs." If you know what you need—for example, relaxation and adventure—you can find many ways of satisfying them, not only going to Hawaii. It may take years to get the money for a trip to Hawaii. You may wish to save for this purpose. However, you may want to meet your needs in the short term. By all means, go to Hawaii, but have options to meet your needs *now*.

The Big Questions

Ask yourself stimulating questions. These questions can enhance your creative dreaming.

(A) If I won the lottery, what would I do with my life? Two years after winning the lottery, what would I do?

(B) If I were to die in some way (out of my control) in six months, how would I want to spend this precious time?

(C) When on my deathbed, as I review my life, do I have any regrets? What keys to my happiness would I share with my family gathered around me? Write this down and share it with a friend or family member.

(D) Someone reads my self-written eulogy at my funeral and it says...

(E) On my tombstone it says...

(F) If I could be successful at anything I choose— if I couldn't fail, if I were GUARANTEED success!—+what would I do now with my life?

Choosing a Path

Brainstorming leads to action steps. Once you have a sense of your needs, pick the top three to five priorities. If you scatter your energy with too many ideas, you'll become overwhelmed and unfocused.

- Pick one set of needs to begin with, such as "I'm traveling for fun, adventure and relaxation". Think of all the ways you can turn these needs into wants or specific ways

of meeting your needs. Brainstorm by yourself and by asking others all the specific
ways to meet your needs for adventure,
fun and relaxation. Put on a page ten or
more ways to meet your needs. Up to now,
you've been stuck on Hawaii. Now your
traveling could be to go to your backyard
for fun, adventure and relaxation, or to a
local spa for the day. Many ideas could
satisfy these needs.

- Then, sort out all your ideas into useful
  and not useful ideas. Which of the ideas
  feels the best, the number one? Use your
  entire body feeling to help you choose
  what you mostly want or love. Don't rely on
  logic only or even less, your critic, which
  may say you don't deserve these needs
  anyway. Logic may tell you " I don't have
  the money". Logically you could wipe out
  Hawaii even when it feels the best for your
  needs. You can work with your logical
  mind to earn the money, or find a way to
  get to Hawaii cheaply. Don't fight with your
  critic or logical mind—just acknowledge
  their presence without agreeing. For now,
  let your good feelings choose the most
  useful ideas. In a moment, we'll work with
  logic and the irrational critic.

Transformation: A New You

After sorting your ideas and picking the most useful of them, you may find yourself highly resistant to doing anything. You hear or feel thoughts like "I've got no money, time or energy". You could feel guilty or fearful that "I don't deserve it, and I don't know how to get there anyway". At this point, you can use your inner and outer allies discussed earlier to help transform these sometimes illogical reasons or illogical thoughts that could sabotage your gifts.

Overcoming or Transforming Self-Sabotage
    — Use the Adventuring: Through Inner Listening chapter to embrace your fears and reassure or soothe yourself. This will help you listen to your intuitive wisdom that sits right underneath the fear. It's ready and waiting to help you if you learn to reassure and not fight your fears.
    — Use your Higher Power to help soothe yourself and give you ideas.
    — Use healthy logic to help counter rigid "all or nothing" thoughts, such as "I can't go because I have no money. That's it". Problem solve to find or earn the money to go to Hawaii. Or choose to visit a spa to get your needs met and not wait to get the money. Getting your needs met is the stuff of listening to your heart and having logic be your ally to find a way to overcome obstacles.
    — See a hypnotherapist to help you heal historical wounds and false beliefs from your childhood that sabotage your dreams.

Perspiration: You In Action

Now that you have done your basic *preparation*, have become *inspired* by your dreaming and brainstorming, and *transformed* your critic into a healthy evaluator, you are ready to perspire a bit with small steps of action.

   – You may wish to take one week in your calendar and plan several small steps to reach your dream. Brainstorm all the small steps you may need to actually meet your need for relaxing fun travel. If you decided on a local spa or hot spring then think of who with, when, how much to spend, where to stay, what to do, how to get there. Over a week's period you could decide to explore options and get a book at the library on local hot springs, or go to the internet with key words and explore.

   – Over the next several weeks, map a general plan and schedule when you're going.

   Slowly the details unfold. A plan of action comes about with baby steps—it's a cinch by the inch and hard by the yard.

Celebration! Learning to Enjoy the Journey

Learning to enjoy the journey of dreaming and the process of getting to your goal is essential. We often focus too much on the result or outcome and not the anticipation or small steps to get there. I want to enjoy wondering about the trip to Hawaii way before hand. I want to imagine what I'll be doing. I want to anticipate and share possibilities with the travel agent.

As with any outcome, a trip or journey may turn out differently than you expected. I once went on a trip to Mexico in college, just as a summer getaway. This trip changed my life. I became fluent in Spanish and taught migrant children for six years in the 1970s. So leaving expectations behind can prepare you for a wonderful change!

Let your dreams unfold with little joys, not just waiting for the big bang at the end: Enjoy the outcome, the thing itself.

Rededication: Re-cycling Your Dream Energy

Take time to celebrate and be thankful and then rededicate yourself to reclaiming old dreams or developing new ones. Keep the creative cycle going again and again as you spiral up and up in your love of life. You may slip back at times with the old critic tapes saying you don't deserve to be happy. You can catch the falling back towards old habits with the help of your inner and outer allies. Life is a continual journey. Happiness is an experience obtained from incrementally moving toward your goals and enjoying your heart's desire.

About This Chapter

*Here are six suggestions or six action steps or six questions to help transform the ideas in this chapter into A **Really Radical Spiritually Adventurous Life**. Write your responses on these pages just as if this were a workbook or on a separate sheet of paper (if you prefer privacy, may want to loan the book to someone, etc.).*

1. What caught your attention or was of particular interest to you in this chapter?

2. Any new ideas or possible adventures you might want to think about after reading this chapter?

3. What have you not thought about that this chapter has brought to your attention?

4. What would be one small step you could do in the next 24 hours to experiment with this chapter?

5. How might you sabotage or resist experimenting, with baby steps, for more adventure in your life (look for information, in this book, that can help to release resistance with _The Ten Step Miracle_ or _Bio-spiritual Focusing_)?

6. What type of additional support might you need to help transform daily life into an amazingly adventurous life? Like- minded friends, groups, a mentor or sponsor? Your own "inner allies" (as explained in this book) or listening to a "Higher wisdom" by various means?

Make a quick list if you like.

**Further Notes, Thoughts
Or Ideas**

"Gratitude is not only the greatest of virtues, but the parent of all others."

– Cicero

CHAPTER 9

Creating A Greater Attitude of Gratitude

The Path To True Inner Peace And Happiness

One of the greatest keys to happiness is the adventure of gratitude. Gratitude is defined by Webster as "the quality of being filled with greatness or grace." Gratitude is an attitude we cultivate with effort and practice over time. It is being thankful for each moment in our lives. It is a lifestyle of blessing each moment for the gift of life we have been given. When you bless each moment or give thanks, a sense of wonder develops about our lives, a sense of feeling connected, whole and complete. Gratitude gives us a feeling of being good enough because, in any given moment, life is good enough. You are good enough—whole and complete. Gratitude is essentially an attitude of appreciating what you have in any moment or experience. It is a substance or energy, like food, that feeds us joy when we focus on being thankful.

Take a moment right now. Close your eyes and think of something small like a pet, a person, a place or event that you really are thankful for. Notice how it feels in your body. Often the outcome of this attitude is a feeling of more joy in the moment.

Gratitude results in a feeling of happiness right now. Gratitude also results in more abundance and prosperity. A grateful heart is like a magnet that attracts more. You get what you believe you deserve. If you believe in lack or scarcity, "I don't have enough" or "I won't be happy unless I have...", you cannot experience joy or contentment in the moment. This does not mean you lack goals or future desires. You work for more in life while being satisfied with the present. How can you have happiness in the future if you can't experience it now? It's a paradox. You learn to balance gratitude in the present and wanting more in the future. Therefore, it is impossible to be truly happy unless you have gratitude in the now.

Balance your life with gratitude for now—the completeness of your life now—with gratitude for your creative goals as you journey to achieve more. Every goal or achievement is best enjoyed by being grateful for the creative process of manifesting it—not just the result or product achieved. For instance, in the writing of this book, I am grateful for the adventure of this process in working with Jim. It took two years of starts and stops and brainstorming and discussion. Who knows what will become of this book? I am truly thankful for this adventure of learning to write and the adventure of the adventure itself. I am also grateful for what I have in my life—wife, children, home, nature and an aging body. I am complete right now, and I am also growing and changing.

Gratitude as Growth

Gratitude is often only associated with good experiences or good events. In fact, gratitude is an attitude of being thankful for the good and perceived bad in life. It does not come from the event. It is how you view events. You might ask if something bad happens in your life—a broken leg or loss of a loved one—how could you possibly be grateful? It's not that you like what is happening in the midst of a small or big tragedy. It is what you choose to learn from the experience.

If your leg is broken and you are mending for three months, maybe you choose to enjoy the down time by reading or developing an inner life of meditation, or you could find creative ways of exercising. You could do isometrics instead. In gratitude you do not deny your grief over the loss of your mobility. You give compassion to your sadness or anger, like you would to a small child. This helps you move through the loss and release your grief. It is the false beliefs of "Life is hopeless" or "I'm helpless" that contribute to a loss of optimistic gratitude or possibilities in the moment. Gratitude can help you out of a prison of hopelessness and helplessness to a place of choices and opportunities.

In every crisis there is an opportunity for growth. If I fail, I can learn forgiveness. What have I learned when I have failed? I failed to complete law school. I spent two years there, but I learned so much. First, I learned I did not want to be an attorney. All my life, I would have wondered or regretted if I had not experienced this schooling. I also am grateful because I learned I prefer relationship counseling, not legal counseling; I prefer right brain intuitive thinking which law school does not promote. I'm grateful, not resentful, for that failure. Gratitude gives us a spiritual peace from lessons learned in the midst of bad times.

Another benefit to gratitude is that it is a magnet to more love and joy. Gratitude releases the chemical endorphin which creates a feeling of more vitality and energy in the body. When we are more vital and alive, we connect to others for more intimacy and also take space for rejuvenation. We set boundaries for alone time and closeness because we know we are good enough being separate or together.

Cultivating Gratitude

How do you develop gratefulness in your life? Gratitude is best cultivated over time by taking small steps. Because we have so much resistance to feeling whole and complete, we must cultivate gratitude for just the adventure of learning to be grateful. Most every one of us has a part of ourselves that is self-critical, or feels unworthy. It is the basic wounding from our childhood and adult traumas. We must bring compassion to this fear and even feel grateful for it. We won't know how joy or intimacy feels unless we feel its opposite—rejection. Again, being grateful for self-rejection doesn't mean we believe it or like it—it means we forgive ourselves for our humanness—our contradictory natures of highs and lows. Gratitude brings us back into balance in our lives.

Practice: Growing Your Gratitude

Here are just a few specific ways of bringing more gratitude into your life. Look at this list and experiment with one of them in the next five minutes. Start small. Add your own ideas. Find a buddy to express your gratitude out loud. Gratitude takes practice.

– Be thankful for your surroundings right now. If you're lying reading in bed, notice all around you. Be thankful for its comfort. Wherever you are sitting or standing, look around and appreciate it right now. Take a few deep breaths and find something to be grateful for in the next five minutes.

– Make and keep a gratitude journal of three to five things a day to scribble down before you sleep or upon awakening to start your day.

– Be thankful for people around you. Start with appreciating loved ones or friends and sharing this gratitude with them. Go next to your enemies or people you dislike and appreciate what they are teaching you. What you intensely dislike in others is often a mirror to what you do not like in yourself. When you appreciate or accept them, or even pray for them, you will release your resentment and heal yourself. Try it.

— Be grateful to your higher power, whatever you conceive that to be—for example, nature, God, the universe.

— Just say "thank you" with emphasis and sincerity during the day to yourself or to others.

— Have a gratitude day. Spend one day a week practicing being thankful at work and home. Notice how your mood changes.

— Look at gratitude as a prayer. Create your own short gratitude prayer or mantra. Memorize it and let it change your life gradually over time.

About This Chapter

*Here are six suggestions or six action steps or six questions to help transform the ideas in this chapter into A **Really Radical Spiritually Adventurous Life**. Write your responses on these pages just as if this were a workbook or on a separate sheet of paper (if you prefer privacy, may want to loan the book to someone, etc.).*

1. What caught your attention or was of particular interest to you in this chapter?

2. Any new ideas or possible adventures you might want to think about after reading this chapter?

3. What have you not thought about that this chapter has brought to your attention?

4. What would be one small step you could do in the next 24 hours to experiment with this chapter?

5. How might you sabotage or resist experimenting, with baby steps, for more adventure in your life (look for information, in this book, that can help to release resistance with <u>The Ten Step Miracle</u> or <u>Bio-spiritual Focusing</u>)?

6. What type of additional support might you need to help transform daily life into an amazingly adventurous life? Like- minded friends, groups, a mentor or sponsor? Your own "inner allies" (as explained in this book) or listening to a "Higher Wisdom" by various means?

Make a quick list if you like.

**Further Notes, Thoughts
Or Ideas**

"When emotions are blocked, they're blind. But when emotions are seen as signposts, we begin to learn from them."

— *Gabriele Rico*

CHAPTER 10

Increasing the Volume of Our Internal Voice –

The Inner GPS for Our Journey

We know that relationships with other people—family, friends, spouse, partner, co-workers, neighbors—require that we communicate. While most of us are comfortable with talking and sharing our ideas or opinions (or that may be an adventure for some!), many of us are still practicing the art of listening. When we don't pay attention to someone (like a child or spouse) at the end of a long work day or when preoccupied with thoughts, often times we are asked "Are you listening to me??" In that instant we are reminded that someone needs our attention. When we tune in to their request, we can be present and aware and ready to listen. We focus on the other. But what about our feelings? Just as it takes effort to nurture relationships with another person, developing an understanding of our feelings takes awareness and conscious commitment to listen...and they want to be heard.

The Jungle of Feelings, Moods and Emotions

Feelings? What kind of feelings? Feelings like "I feel hungry" or "I feel tired"? Or, "I feel anxious, worried or scared, mad or sad, happy, glad, good or bad"? Stuff like that? Yes, all of it. In fact, when most people are asked to name as many feeling words as they can think of the list is quite short. So here is a short list of feeling words many people fail to mention: exhausted, confused, ecstatic, guilty, suspicious, hysterical, frustrated, confident, embarrassed, mischievous, disgusted, enraged, ashamed, cautious, smug, depressed, overwhelmed, hopeful, lonely, love-struck, jealous, bored, surprised, shocked, shy...

The first thing that needs to be said about this radically broad topic is that there are various schools of thought about how to generally deal with our feelings—for instance, to accept them or not accept them, to reject them or ignore them, or to listen to them and learn from them, etc. Often, mental health practitioners and others who wrote about what to do with our feelings disagree with which approach or methodology is most effective, valid, or useful.

What Is __Not__ Feeling Our Feelings

There are several examples of differing ways to deal with one's feelings:

- Define all feelings as either positive or negative (good or bad, helpful or hurtful, sinful or pure, loving or selfish...) and only allow the "good" or the "positive" or the "healthy" feelings to enter your consciousness.
- Not allow feelings to take over your life. If you do, they will only turn into self-pity and lead to depression and debilitating moods. Instead, get busy and do something useful (clean out a closet), do something fun, focus on helping others, or go to the mall and practice some "retail therapy".
- Numb out or stuff any and all feelings you don't like. Use whatever drug of choice that works best. It could be ice cream, chocolate, pizza, television, surfing the internet, computer gaming, over-working, over-committing and, of course, booze, pills or a hundred other things.

Some may be all too familiar; they are common ways of coping that may lull us into believing we have dealt with the feelings.

There are many other ways to avoid "feeling" our feelings. Some of these ways may even be unintentional or dealt with unconsciously. It's quite easy to avoid looking at what we are feeling by dumping it on someone else. It's sometimes easier to say to someone, "Look, I want to be honest with you, I've got to tell you the truth. When you said (or did or didn't say or didn't do) it upset me (or disappointed me or hurt me or....) and please don't do it again." This could be called the blame game. What I'm feeling is someone else's fault so I don't have to deal with why or what I felt had to do with me. Other ways of avoiding unpleasant feelings is to say, "I'm just telling you what's on my mind..." or "You need to know that..." or "I need to tell you I'm feeling..."

There are times when saying exactly those words would be very appropriate especially if the situation happened before and the feelings it produced had been fully experienced and allowed to reveal any insights they might have been able to offer. Plus, if someone wants to tell you something that starts with words like these, it doesn't necessarily mean you are the problem or you did anything wrong. If the intention is to heal your feelings, not to blame, this is appropriate.

Many of us haven't had the chance to learn other, healthier ways to deal with our feelings. But there is a better way.

A Better Way: Befriending Our Feelings
It is our belief, as expressed throughout this book, that all of our "feelings", "moods" and "emotions" (these three words are used inter-changeably for our purposes here) are important and are worth being acknowledged, listened to, and can help us identify who we are and what we want or need to be happy and fulfilled during our time on this planet.

We believe that our feelings can be our friends and we can welcome them and thank them for showing up and telling us their stories.

We also think that as human beings we are one of the highest forms of life on Earth. Being able to experience our own emotional awareness is a God-given gift and to not feel our feelings, even when they are painful at times, is to deny a part of the specialness that human beings have been given. The problem is, in our society and in many others, the "Driver's Manual" for how to use these feelings of ours got lost a very long time ago, and we don't have a clue about how to properly make them work for us as they are capable of doing. The purpose of this chapter is to offer a possible "Quick Start" guide to the missing Driver's Manual.

The Only Way Out Is Through

This phrase, "The Only Way Out Is Through", captures the essence of what we believe is the path to learning about what our feelings can teach us or how our feelings can help us. What this phrase means is we cannot skip over, go around, deny or distract ourselves from going *through* possible difficult feelings, moods or emotions that have come to our attention from a reoccurring insight, thought, observation, perception or idea.

Whatever has triggered these reoccurring thoughts or ideas may seem too unimportant or silly to be explored, but the feelings behind or accompanying them could be of real significance.

Refusing to allow such feelings to be uncovered and listened to or looked at, especially if they seem potentially troublesome or fearful, could likely get worse over time and cause further injury or pain. This is the reason for the saying, The Only Way Out Is Through.

It is as if the longer we ignore our feelings, the more they will try to get our attention. Slowly they may become bolder in a variety of ways. At first, our stronger or more important feelings may try to get our attention by causing stress somewhere in our bodies. It could be increasing stiffness in our neck or shoulders. It could be little headaches that become more frequent or increase in strength. It could be more irritability or a gradually noticeable loss of patience especially about things that never used to bother us as much as they do now. Before long, it is, perhaps, as if there is something inside our minds that is shouting at us but we don't know what it is. But there is a way to find out...a way to listen.

Every Body Knows

One of the greatest and most important adventures of all is learning to go inside and listen to your body's wisdom. By listening to your body's sensations, such as tightness or tension, feelings will emerge like a child speaking to you, telling you what it needs or wants. You can learn to pay attention, non-judgmentally, to sensations that uncover feelings and needs. For example, tightness in the neck is often a zone of suppressed anger. The anger indicates a need for space, freedom or self-respect. If you reach for alcohol, sugar, or the nearest aspirin to cover up the tension, you'll numb the wisdom of the body's needs.

The body's intuitive wisdom is essential for self-esteem and self-care, and if you're on the road to self-care through inner listening, you will be better able to love and care for others.

Tuning In: The Process of Focusing

Over thirty years ago, a process called Focusing was uncovered to help us go within and listen. Focusing was invented by Eugene Gendlin in the 1960's. In the 70's and 80's, Edwin McMahon and Peter Campbell added to Gendlin's work and created Biospritual Focusing.

Here's how Focusing works…

Some days I wake up and I'm feeling a general malaise, a fog, or a tension in my body. I can't quite put my finger on it—tightness in my neck, tension in my jaw. I'm tense, irritable, but I don't know what it's about. This mood is an old friend, familiar—I know it. In the past I've ignored it, repressed it or tried to numb it with food. (I still do it at times.) Ignoring it leads to temporary relief as I gulp down my coffee and eat my sugar-coated cereal. Soon this temporary relief fades, and my mood leaks out onto my family. I'm snapping at my kids or wife for small things that really don't mean much, or over-react and yell when things aren't important.

Then, I feel sad. Instead of a quick fix, I need to explore what this mood is all about. What am I needing? What are the gifts in this mood that paradoxically are trying to teach me something? Feelings and sensations in my body are trying to send a message—"Pay attention to me!", almost like a child wanting to be loved and heard. What are you going to do, Adult Richard? **I decide to go within, to Focus.**

Focusing invites me to love and listen to the tension and let it tell its story. Gendlin called the stories "felt senses". By listening to my feelings and sensations, I learn the Golden Rule: Love thy neighbor as thyself. I learn that healthy self-love is a prerequisite to caring for others. I learn that inside these moods or felt senses is a vein of gold to be tapped, to be mined, that unveils a wealth of love and peace.

Focusing as a Path to Wisdom

What are the benefits of this inner Focusing adventure? Multi-fold! As I listen to tightness, my body felt mind shares symbols that reflect a need for slowing down. I hear anger, and a need for space or relaxation. I hear intuitive phrases like respect me, hold me and love me. I connect to inner meaning and passion and purpose, that my logical mind or left-brain cannot fathom.

I could still ignore these words and feelings. I have a choice to own them or not. I choose to listen and act with gentle, loving self-care and provide for the needs by scheduling a massage, taking time to wander aimlessly, playing the guitar, sitting quietly, or planning for the future.

Focusing is not a new process for connecting with inner wisdom. Throughout the United States and the world, people have been focusing individually and together. Focusing has six major steps, but is neither dogmatic nor rigid. It is an adventure of going inward and listening to moods and sensations by first growing quiet, connecting to the body and just noticing without trying to fix or change anything. So often we try to figure out or analyze our uncomfortable feelings and then get rid of them. In Focusing, we learn to slowly listen with love to the intuitive wisdom within the story of our emotions. It is truly a rewarding adventure.

The Six Steps of Focusing

Step One: I simply close my eyes and gently turn inward, noticing without judgment my body's sensations or feelings. Maybe I scan my body for a minute, head to toe.

Step Two: Focus on what feels "hot" or "prickly" inside. Maybe there is more than one set of sensations. I feel a knot in my stomach, but I also feel a ball of tension in my neck and jaw. I decide to pay attention to the tension in my neck and jaw. If I try to focus on too many issues at once, I overwhelm myself. By choosing a "Number 1" issue or feeling, I open a doorway for all the rest to unfold.

Step Three: I continue to listen and not force or figure it out. I ask my body, gently, if it's okay to even

feel this ball of tension. I hear an angry "NO!"—
I'm resistant to it. What a surprise. A road block?
A dead-end? No, it's a doorway into the tension
and anger; this resistance is part of the story of this
adventure. Can I be with this resistance and anger?
Can I spend some time listening to it? "Yes", I hear
from my feeling mind. It's okay to spend time with
it.

Step Four: I listen to this anger as I would a friend
or a child, with compassion, not trying to fix or
change the anger. I give caring and empathy to
this feeling so it will tell its story, what it needs. This
comforts the anger. I do not have to like the anger
or agree with it. I'm simply acknowledging it with
compassionate curiosity. I create a safe place for it
to tell me its story.

Step Five: Now I let go into this anger, listen to the
anger, waiting. I let it express itself from its point
of view. I hear anger saying I should be above this
by now. I should know more and be more patient
by now. I ask, "What do you need to know from
me, anger, that would help you?" I hear "forgiveness". It's okay to be imperfect. It's okay to recycle.
It's a process: remembering and forgetting. I hear
the word "patience". I experience a release, a shift,
a calming in my body. I hear "Thank you for listening." It is like sitting with a friend and listening
without force or advice.

As the Focusing continues, I notice more sensations to be explored. More anger appears. This
time I sense it in my back. Again, I give it more

compassion. As I feel my anger in a caring nurturing way, more messages are revealed. "Space, wandering, less schedule, less rigidity, doing nothing, wandering". I experience more release.

I ask if there is a small step or idea to help meet these needs. I hear my inner loving intuitive voice say, "Just get in your car and drive without a specific destination, smell the flowers, no calendar, no schedule." I realize my life is out of balance—too much scheduling.

Step Six: I am ready to stop. It's not all finished; there is some residue. I caringly ask, "How do you need me to be with you until I can come back?" I hear, "Hold me and check in with me." I check in now and discover my neck and jaw tension have softened and the malaise or fog has lifted. I say, "Thank you, body, for once again teaching me. Thank you for another adventure in listening to my inner wisdom by going underneath and inside the resistance." As I care for the resistance, it peels away like an onion to reveal inner needs and intuitive ideas. As I connect and listen to my body, I connect to God, wisdom or higher power in the universe.

What an adventure! What a gift!

About This Chapter

Here are six suggestions or six action steps or six questions to help transform the ideas in this chapter into A **Really Radical Spiritually Adventurous Life**. *Write your responses on these pages just as if this were a workbook or on a separate sheet of paper (if you prefer privacy, may want to loan the book to someone, etc.).*

1. What caught your attention or was of particular interest to you in this chapter?

2. Any new ideas or possible adventures you might want to think about after reading this chapter?

3. What have you not thought about that this chapter has brought to your attention?

4. What would be one small step you could do in the next 24 hours to experiment with this chapter?

5. How might you sabotage or resist experimenting, with baby steps, for more adventure in your life (look for information, in this book, that can help to release resistance with The Ten Step Miracle or Bio-spiritual Focusing)?

6. What type of additional support might you need to help transform daily life into an amazingly adventurous life? Like- minded friends, groups, a mentor or sponsor? Your own "inner allies" (as explained in this book) or listening to a "Higher Wisdom" by various means?

Make a quick list if you like.

**Further Notes, Thoughts
Or Ideas**

"As I progress in the spiritual life, God increases as I decrease. It's more than just being detached; it's as if God is absorbing the self."

– *Bernadette Roberts*

CHAPTER 11

Accepting Life on Life's Terms —
A Really Radical Spiritual Adventure

As we start finding new ways of making the various individual and separate parts of our lives more adventurous, our entire life begins to feel like it's becoming just one big, all-encompassing adventure. Perhaps the most wonderful spiritual gift we can receive or the highest form of spiritual wisdom we can have is the awareness that our whole life is, ultimately, the greatest adventure of all.

Yet sometimes life can feel *too* adventurous. We lose a job…someone breaks a promise…the car breaks down… . During times like these, we can forget that life offers lessons and gifts beyond our immediate understanding. One of the best ways to come back to balance and find the joy in the adventure of life is to practice accepting life on life's terms.

Here is an excerpt from pages 178-179 of the book *Alcoholics Anonymous*. (This is the book fondly referred to as "The Big Book" by men and women in 12-step groups worldwide.)

"...Acceptance is the answer to all my problems today. When I am disturbed, it is because I find some place, thing or situation—some fact of my life—is unacceptable to me and I can find no serenity until I accept that person, place, thing or situation as being exactly the way it is...at this moment. Unless I accept life completely on life's terms, I cannot be happy. I need to concentrate not so much on what needs to be changed in the world as on what needs to be changed in me and in my attitudes."

Training ourselves to do this is no easy matter and doing so may well be a life-long adventure.

I was born in the Midwest and brought up to believe life "should" be like a Norman Rockwell painting. This was in spite of having had parents who were nothing like what Rockwell's paintings portrayed. (If you don't know who Norman Rockwell was, check him out on the internet.) Maybe I looked at too many *Life Magazine* covers.

Nevertheless, I still have to this day an image in my head of how people "should" act, look, and think that is completely out of touch with our very different present day society. Accepting life as it actually is in the world around me is a continuing challenge. What I know is that acceptance does not have to mean approval. They are not one and the same. But without acceptance of what is actually in the here and now, resentment will thrive, and I will not know peace or serenity over anything that troubles me.

A <u>Revised</u> Serenity Prayer

This is a revised version of the Serenity Prayer which I heard some time ago and it stuck with me: "God, grant me the serenity to accept the things I cannot change <u>in me, in others and in the world around me</u>, courage to change the things I can <u>in me, in others and in the world around me</u>, and the wisdom to know the difference."

Accepting the New Normal

Times change. Things change. What we've come to think of as normal—sometimes slowly, sometimes quickly—is no longer normal. For example, check-in at airports after 9-11 will never be the same again. The old normal is suddenly gone. Gripe and complain all you want, but a new normal has taken over. Accept it or resent it, but the old normal is gone forever. This new normal is sure to change again to another new normal, requiring us to go through another round of acceptance...or not.

Since the publication of the first edition of this book in 1999, I (Jim) was diagnosed with multiple sclerosis. Since that time, walking normally was no longer normal. It is for me now the old normal. There is nothing I or medical science can do about it.

Accepting this has not been easy. I'm still working at it. The new normal isn't yet normal enough to feel normal. But staying stuck to the old normal and hating every minute of the new normal is never going to bring me happiness, peace or resolution. The only reasonable course of action over this thing I do not have the personal power to change is acceptance. In this case, acceptance, for me, is definitely a process, not a simple snap decision, but I have many more days of feeling relaxed and at peace about my new normal than not.

Is this an adventure? Absolutely…if I allow myself to think in those terms. It's part of my life's adventure. Life is taking me places I never planned to go, over hills I never thought I could climb, through valleys I never thought I would see, showing me things I never imagined possible. One day soon I'm sure I'll be able to say I'm grateful for this latest segment of my life of adventure made possible by accepting life on life's terms.

It's not always easy. In fact it's often damn difficult, especially if it involves the loss of something of great importance, something you had hope for, or someone you loved. No matter how difficult, acceptance of life on life's terms is always necessary before real healing or positive change can begin.

This idea is expressed best, I think, in the following excerpts from a story of an unknown author. The title is:

The Road Of Life
"At first it seemed to me as though life were rather like riding on a tandem bike with God in back help-

ing me pedal. I was in control. I knew the way. Life was rather boring, but it was predictable. I always made sure we took the shortest distance between two points. I don't remember exactly when it was that God suggested we change places, but I can tell you life has not been the same since.

When God took over the lead, we stopped taking shortcuts. He, in fact, started taking us on unexpected long cuts, up mountains and through rocky places at breakneck speeds. It was all I could do to hang on. Even though it looked to me like madness, He just said, 'Keep pedaling'! I was anxious and worried and I asked, 'Where are you taking me'? He just laughed and didn't answer... and I had to learn how to trust.

I forgot my boring life and entered into the adventure. When I'd say I was scared, He'd lean back and touch my hand. He took me to people with gifts I need, gifts of healing, acceptance and joy. They were gifts to take on my journey, my God's and mine!

When we were off again, God said, 'Give the gifts away; they are extra baggage, too much weight.' So I did, to the people we met, and I found that in giving I received, and still our burden was light. I did not trust Him at first to be in control of my life. I thought He'd wreck it, but I've discovered He knows bike secrets, knows how to make it bend to take sharp corners, jump to clear high rocks and fly to shorten rough passages.

I've learned to shut up and just pedal. Even in the strangest places our adventure takes us, I'm beginning to enjoy the view and the cool breeze on my face as my travel guide, God, leads the way. Now and then, when I think I know which road is best or which way we should go, He just smiles and says... 'Keep pedaling'."

A Gradual Process

Participating in our life in such a way that everything we encounter is thought of as being part of one, grand, overall adventure is, I think, the essence of spiritual living. However, for most of us, allowing God (or whatever we call our Higher Power) to lead us on the pathways of our life is usually a gradual, scary, back and forth process. Initially, we may only let God take control of matters when the situation or circumstance we are facing is so overpowering that we have no other choice.

Over a period of time and with perhaps only a small measure of faith, we may begin to trust our Higher Power more and more to show us the way or lead us to a destination we never expected. This is where we truly enter the adventure of a spiritual life. It's usually a gradual process to be sure.

Here are a few questions to think about that may facilitate our willingness to risk having a more spiritually adventurous life.

Practice: Writing Your Story of Surrender

Think about a time in your life when you put something in God's hands and allowed God to take the lead.

- What was the situation or circumstance about?
- Did God choose a path or a destination different than what you would have chosen?
- Was God's route longer, rockier, and more uncertain than you had planned?
- At times, was it all you could do to just hang on and keep pedaling?
- What surprises came from this experience, if any?
- What valuable lessons did you learn?
- What unexpected gifts did this experience bring to you?
- How could this experience help you to help others?
- How was this experience in any way an unanticipated positive adventure?

Writing out the answers to these questions for times when we have let God steer us on our road of life can be of great value. There is often something tremendously therapeutic (and mystically divine) in writing about how God shapes and fashions our life's journey when we stop trying to be in control so much. Furthermore, writing out answers to questions like these not only gives us a written record of where we've been but helps us see how we got to where we're at now and can even help prepare us for where we may be headed. It's kind of a travel log of this great adventure called life.

About This Chapter

Here are six suggestions or six action steps or six questions to help transform the ideas in this chapter into A **Really Radical Spiritually Adventurous Life**. Write your responses on these pages just as if this were a workbook or on a separate sheet of paper (if you prefer privacy, may want to loan the book to someone, etc.).

1. What caught your attention or was of particular interest to you in this chapter?

2. Any new ideas or possible adventures you might want to think about after reading this chapter?

3. What have you not thought about that this chapter has brought to your attention?

4. What would be one small step you could do in the next 24 hours to experiment with this chapter?

5. How might you sabotage or resist experimenting, with baby steps, for more adventure in your life (look for information, in this book, that can help to release resistance with The Ten Step Miracle or Bio-spiritual Focusing)?

6. What type of additional support might you need to help transform daily life into an amazingly adventurous life? Like- minded friends, groups, a mentor or sponsor? Your own "inner allies" (as explained in this book) or listening to a "Higher Wisdom" by various means?

Make a quick list if you like.

Further Notes, Thoughts Or Ideas

There is nothing wrong with having material things.
But, material things do not help achieve a deep sense of happiness.

— *Martin Seligman*

CHAPTER 12

The Ten Minute Miracle –

The Adventure Of Uncovering Our Needs Right Now

The 10 Minute Miracle is a series of sentence completions which when done rapidly—out loud or in writing—will guide you to a treasure within. Sentence completion or prompts are beginnings of sentences that guide the student to deeper and deeper wisdom when he or she writes quickly and without analyzing the responses. I (Richard)have used this spiritual tool for ten years with huge benefits for myself and my clients.

Martin Seligman, author of *Authentic Happiness*, has proved through scientific research that outer circumstances in our lives—money, material things—will only bring small increases of happiness or fulfillment in our lives,

Uncovering the Layers

When Ed hit bottom, he was willing to face his inner critic's fears and childhood wounding that said he must be a success or he would be a nothing, a failure, unworthy. His fear of failure had been planted in him as the oldest of five children who could only please his father by succeeding in school and sports. He grew up not enjoying the moment and could only be happy if he could achieve his goals. Even then, when he did achieve them, his moments of celebration were very fleeting. In his adult life, while succeeding in outward forms, Ed was still not happy. Every success led to trying to achieve something more—a never ending cycle of boredom, overworking, not being present to the happiness right now.

After a lifetime of frustrated attempts at happiness, Ed was open to doing the Ten Minute Miracle: sentences that allowed him to go deep within, to access an inner knowing that was already there.

Are you willing to listen and trust the divine guidance that lies within you? Like Ed's, the conditioning of your childhood will keep you in a constant struggle of waiting to be happy in the future and not living in the precious present where you can attain divine guidance and happiness. The Ten Minute Miracle is a process, somewhat like peeling an onion—layers upon layers of opening, maybe even crying a bit as people do when they slice open onions. Or if you prefer, an artichoke—the prickly leaves of an artichoke, peeling them away to get to the heart. Unfortunately most people, living an artichoke life never get to the heart. Ed had hit bottom, and was willing to go inside instead of relying excessively on external forms of happiness. It is a choice, and some people will never make this choice, and will continue to live their lives based on the inner critic, which says "I'm only okay if I succeed or please or try to control things outside of me."

What it takes is a willingness to face fear, even the fear of your own joy and happiness. We often have layers of fear—fear of the fear itself, and then even fear of the joy that lies right within us, ready to guide us if we are only willing to claim our birthright. We have become accustomed to familiar feelings and are afraid of changes and the unknown.

Like Ed, we are all conditioned to struggle and to believe that our happiness lies only in the future, not in the present. So we all strive for more—more things, more success, more love—all outside of us. It is never enough to fully satisfy us. But when we balance our external lives with an inner life using the Ten Minute Miracle and other tools, we can find the harmony, and the inner balance, that often alludes us.

Ed's old strategies for quick fix happiness no longer worked. He was willing to make the effort, to choose one day at a time, to go inside using the Ten Minute Miracle. There are so few practical spiritual tools and signposts that help us and allow us to do the inner work. It just takes a willingness to do five simple steps for a miracle to occur. And as I taught Ed, I will teach you now.

The 10 Minute Miracle Steps
Here is a summary of the five steps:
1. Scan the Body and Call On Allies
2. Pick a Number One Issue or Feeling
3. Nurture the Number One
4. Listen Through Rapid Automatic Writing or Vocalizing Responses
5. Give Thanks

Step One: Scan the Body and Call On Allies
The first step is to simply notice the body with the help of inner imaginary allies. This step before the uncovering of essence allows us to form a safe embrace of feelings and issues which we normally run away from through too much food or alcohol or shopping, or any other excess that numbs our emotions. But numbing or avoiding our emotions, while providing a quick fix or a short-term release, only allows those authentic feelings to build up and turn into moods of panic, rage, depression, boredom, jealousy. It's through embracing the emotions and even our dark moods that will allow them to release and guide us to the treasure within.

So right now, take the first step. The first step, again, is to notice the body. Go right down the body...head, neck and shoulders—just sensing, curious, no judgment, not trying to change or fix anything...arms and hands and torso...slowly just sensing, scanning down the body...for about a minute. Maybe you notice body sensations of tension or tightness, or a flow, a calm...whatever you notice, simply observe and witness with compassion and tenderness. If there is a sensation or feeling in the body that is upsetting, try not to change it or judge it. Simply accept it without having to like it. Acceptance does not mean that you have to approve of or like the feeling. Just know that inside the sensation or feeling there is a treasure leading you to possible guidance or inner peace.

This first step is a meditation in itself. Closing your eyes, simply scanning down the body to just notice the sensations and feelings. You can keep your eyes open, but it's best to avoid external visual distractions by closing them. As you do this body scan, if you notice further resistance coming to you—an inner critic thought, or a feeling of tightening or contracting—simply notice this resistance as well. You may experience simply a flow in your body, a calming effect. Whatever you notice, just accept it without judging or analyzing.

To aid you in the body scan and first embrace of sensations, I want you to think of an ally or two to create a sense of safety, because when we go inside, we often meet feelings or emotions that we have rejected or pushed away due to family rules from childhood about not trusting oneself or one's own emotions as inner guidance. We all learn the codependent rules from our dysfunctional families of "don't feel your emotions—don't talk about them and don't trust your intuitive knowing about them."

Your allies can be anything that guides you to a sense of safety, peace, beauty, or comfort—a beloved pet, a loving person in your life, a loving, colored light surrounding you like a blanket of love. You can also think of a phrase or word like "peace" or "love" or the lyrics or a song or melody that can bring you to this sense of safety. By using this person, place, animal, music, or affirmation, you enhance your ability to be with difficult emotions or sensations that you normally avoid and thereby do not access the wisdom within. I cannot emphasize enough the need to use allies when you do this work. We often need friends, spiritual guides, or mentors as external allies to help us go inside, but developing your own internal allies enhances the times when you cannot use the support of others.

Every spiritual tradition known to man has used spirit guides or allies on their journey within. In Asian cultures, loving ancestors long deceased are guides for the living. Native Americans used animals to aid their spiritual journeys. So these practices are not new. It is simply finding your own way—and there is no single right way—to accessing this warm embrace or your emotional life. Almost anything will do—something that connects you to love, a calming... song, a prayer, a real or imaginary place that connects you to safety and love. This caring feeling presence in your body will embrace hurting places and allow them to tell their story in an internal safety while uncovering the deep guidance and wisdom within, inside and under the pain. The cause of our suffering is not so much the pain itself, but the resistance to it which compounds the problem.

When you do this first step of body scan and gathering allies, let go of the outcome. The thought of your allies is enough. If you do not release any tension or become calmer in doing this, it's okay. Throughout the whole process, through all of the steps, you must let go of the outcome. It's on inner guidance's time, not ours. We cannot force a result: that will only create more resistance, which comes from our inner critic wanting something to happen now, rather than being patient and open to divine wisdom's time, not ours.

As you go down the body, with your allies to help, tell each part of your body that you're here for it—your heart, your stomach, your arms, your hands... Notice how it feels when you give love to each part of your body. Very seldom do we pay attention. Each part of our body wants to be loved and held by you.

If you find it difficult to use allies, don't use them at all. You are your own best ally, ultimately.

Once you've scanned your body, put your hand to your heart, and thank your allies; the thought of your allies is enough. Again, if you do not have a body effect of calming while doing this, it is the act of learning to listen and to scan and to be open to your allies that is most important. The thought of your allies there with you—helping and accepting you unconditionally—is enough. The first step is crucial for the next four steps of the Ten Minute Miracle.

Step Two: Pick a "Number One" Issue or Feeling

The next step is to ask your body "What is the Number One issue or problem or feeling for me right now?" You may be aware of an upset in your life and use that issue or feeling. Or, if you're not sure, just ask yourself, "What needs to be heard right now?", what is hot or prickly in a body way? Or "What is keeping me from feeling really good right now?" Something will come to you—an issue, or just a feeling or body sensation. It could be a vague feeling, or something very specific, something big, something small. You don't have to have an upset in advance of using this tool. Just ask your body; it will tell you. Just trust that whatever issue comes to you when you ask your body to pick something will be the outer part of the onion or the prickly part of the artichoke. That's okay—that's the beginning, the opening.

If there are two or three issues, just pick one—maybe the hottest. Pick one that you can be with right now without too much resistance. Ask the feeling, like it is an upset child within you, if you can spend time with it. If it says no, ask it if you can be with the no. If further resistance comes, don't force it. Put it aside if there is too much resistance for

144

now. Put it aside for another day, or until it is open to you and feels safer. It is important to not force or push yourself.

Once you have picked an issue, something you can be with right now, it's then on to the third step. So take time, as Ed did, to let your body pick an issue right. Stop reading, close your eyes, or just listen to your body and ask the question: "What is keeping me from feeling really good right now? What's keeping me from feeling more alive, freer, happier, right now?"

Step Three: Nurture the Number One
The next step of the Ten Minute Miracle is simply to nurture whatever comes, whatever the Number One is, with the help of your inner allies. Imagine your inner allies around you, supporting you—the animal or the person or the place—whatever you chose in the first step. You and your allies are a team, together, to hold this feeling or issue in a loving, embracing way. The key is not to analyze or try to figure out what the problem or issue is trying to tell you, but to let the *feeling* or *body sensation* tell you. To do this, you must become like a mother to a child and not give advice or analyze, but simply be there, listening, nurturing, and opening to whatever comes to you. You might use the words "its okay to feel this, body. Allies and I are here, listening." Again, avoid any criticism or wondering why you feel this. Just go into an acceptance, so that it can open up and tell you its story of pain, to

release it—and maybe even tell you what it needs for you to do for it to let go of this pain or underlying issue or problem.

When you nurture it, you create a safe container to allow these feelings that possibly have been suppressed for your entire life to start opening up to the miracle sentences of the next step.

Step Four: Listen Through Rapid Automatic Writing or Vocalizing Responses

Start either writing the sentence completions from the following pages, or writing rapidly two or three word responses to as many of the miracle sentence prompts as possible, skipping when nothing comes. Or if you prefer, you can vocalize your responses out loud. Just let whatever comes out, pop up, not analyzing or stopping to ponder or figure out why you said what you said. So say these prompts out loud or write them out; skip the prompts if nothing comes up. You may only complete half of them—it's okay. Some may not apply.

After you're done with the sentence prompts, there will be time to analyze, evaluate and problem solve. But for now, there is no right answer. You cannot flunk this process. You do not have to believe what pops out of your mind. Some of the messages that come will be from your inner critic. Some will be intuitive guidance. At the end, you will know which will be the helpful phrases or popups, because they will resonate as a calming, inner serenity. Just let go and trust that there is a deep spiritual wisdom within you.

About 90% of the time, something comes out of the Ten Minute Miracle to guide us to more inner peace and happiness in our decision making in relationships, career, or whatever aspect of your life is troubling you right now. Allow the miracles to work within you and not force or expect an answer. Again, it is like peeling that onion, and the layers come off slowly, gradually, getting to the inner part of the onion which is an open space. If you cut an onion in half, there's an inner space of peace within that onion, just like the heart of the artichoke.

So if you do this whole process in ten minutes, something may come to you. But don't give up if nothing comes to you at the first sitting. We live in a quick fix culture which says "It must happen *now*." But with patience, over time, something will come to you. Do these exercises at least six times before you give up. There is a lot of repetition because our psyche is like this onion of layers that has to be slowly peeled away with safety and a warm embrace.

Step Five: Learning's and Give Thanks
The final Step

After you complete the Ten Minute Miracle, notice your body. Sometimes there is an easing, a slight release or calming. Remember how it felt when you picked this particular issue, this Number One. Sit with your eyes closed and notice any shift to serenity. If there is not a shift, remember, it's okay.

You can't force it. If your inner critic starts judging or tells you that you failed, tell your critic "Thank you for sharing" but don't believe what it tells you. This is a skill which these sentence prompts guide you to going deep within. This is a skill we have never been taught in our entire lives, so you must be patient as you learn to go within in the first four steps—body scan and allies, picking a number one, nurturing it, and then, by writing or saying out loud, letting the sensation tell its story and leading to a treasure within.

If something came to you, give thanks—give thanks to your allies and your body knowing helping you. It's almost as if you and your allies and the warm embrace of love, is guiding you deep into the body to access an even deeper love, a love that we've long forgotten from childhood. So give thanks, if a word or phrase comes from the writing or the vocalizations that helps you to release to more inner peace or happiness. Or if nothing comes, give thanks, too; give thanks for the willingness to go inside, to pay attention. And then, with the patience to come back at another time—maybe in ten minutes, maybe in half an hour, maybe the next day—something will come. Trust that something will come from your inner self if you're only willing to use the Ten Minute Miracle.

When Ed used these steps, he found a tension and tightness in his neck and shoulders, a burden of having to be worthy only if he could succeed that had built up in his body, somewhat like armor.

By using his allies and his own loving embrace, he held tension—this was his Number One. By doing the miracle sentence prompts, he heard the old false beliefs and messages and then right underneath these false messages was an intuitive guidance system helping him to release and to know that he was okay whether he succeeded or not. It told him that happiness had to come from within, balanced with going for what he really wanted externally. Slowly, Ed began to build an inner life of knowing that outer success must be balanced with inner wisdom. The wisdom guided Ed to take action in terms of more creative activities in his life, of enjoying the processes of painting and photography, things he had done as a child and had forgotten long ago.

Ed is no longer suffering from depression or panic attacks. He is on the road to enjoying his life more each day, and he has developed a daily practice of inner listening thanks to the 10 Minute Miracle and other forms of meditation. Ed writes down words or phrases that come to him from the inner prompts. He also uses any action steps to set boundaries in his life and to have healthier relationships with his family and friends and loved ones.

So I now challenge you to practice the 10 Minute Miracle. Are you willing? Are you willing to choose a life of more inner peace and happiness? Or do you want to continue to struggle with the suffering that has been passed down through generations of your family from one parent to the next, unconsciously, through the conditioned mind? You can choose today, one day at a time, to release the suffering. If you have difficulty taking this challenge or are too afraid, then do the 10 Minute Miracle on your fear of even feeling happier, or the fear of doing this process, the fear of trusting that there is a guiding essence within you. Even *that* will open you up to deeper happiness.

A Wish For You

Ultimately, there is no right way of using the Ten Minute Miracle. Experiment when and how you use these sentence completions. Do them at least six times on any subject, not just once and quitting. It may take a few sets of completions to get accustomed to a new tool. Very few people rode a bicycle their first time with any sense of balance. But after a while, it flowed.

Like learning to ride a bicycle, practice is key to becoming comfortable. This process may take 20 minutes the first few times, but with practice you'll need only 10 minutes or so. Repeat the sentence completions as outlined the first six times, then change the process or even the prompts as you wish. If you can't or don't like writing, say them aloud to a friend or to yourself in the mirror. Some of my clients keep a copy of the prompts at their bedside so they can use the practice as a meditation guidance in the morning or as a means to release the monkey mind or inner critic before going to sleep at night. Other clients who suffered from sleep disturbances use the Ten Minute Miracle and sleep soundly without other sleep aides.

Believe that you can do it. Believe the guidance within. Believe in miracles. I wish you well in using this practical tool of spiritual guidance.

The Ten Minute Miracle:
The Practice

Now let go, and let inner guidance unfold.

1. Body Scan and Allies
2. Pick a Number One Issue or Feeling
3. Nurture the Number One
4. Now complete the following sentence prompts rapidly (best done in writing, or vocalizing out loud).

The issue or feeling is

_____

The issue or feeling is

_____

The real issue or feeling is

_____

The issue or feeling really is

_____

The real issue or feeling is

_____

****

And what I'm feeling is

_____

And I'm also feeling

_____

And what I'm really feeling is

_____

And what I'm mad about is

_____

What angers me is

_____

What I truly need is

_____

And I also need

_____

What saddens me is

_____

What hurts is

_____

What I truly need is

_____

What I need to know is

_____

What I need to tell myself is

_____

What scares me is

_____

What I'm afraid of is

_____

What I'm really afraid of is

_____

This fear reminds me of growing up when

_____

To reassure myself I need to know

_____

To comfort this fear I need to know

_____

What I really need is

_____

From deep inner wisdom I know

_____

What is unacceptable to me is

_____

What needs to change here is

_____

What I tell myself that is not helpful is

_____

The price I pay is

_____

By staying stuck, I don't have to

_____

The benefit of staying stuck is

_____

What I need to learn to do differently is

_____

But if I do, what I'm afraid of is

_____

This fear reminds me of growing up when

_____

To heal this fear I need to know that

_____

From my inner wisdom I know

_____

What I need to tell myself is that

_____

One small step I'm willing to take is

_____

What I could do differently is

_____

What I would request from my partner is

_____

One positive step I ask my partner to do is

_____

I'm willing to forgive myself for

_____

I'm willing to forgive my partner for

_____

I love and appreciate myself for being willing to

_____

I also appreciate myself for

_____

I love and appreciate my partner for

_____

I also appreciate my partner for

_____

What I learned in doing this exercise is

_____

What I also learned is

_____

The last thing I want to say is

_____

About This Chapter

*Here are six suggestions or six action steps or six questions to help transform the ideas in this chapter into A **Really Radical Spiritually Adventurous Life**. Write your responses on these pages just as if this were a workbook or on a separate sheet of paper (if you prefer privacy, may want to loan the book to someone, etc.).*

1. What caught your attention or was of particular interest to you in this chapter?

2. Any new ideas or possible adventures you might want to think about after reading this chapter?

3. What have you not thought about that this chapter has brought to your attention?

4. What would be one small step you could do in the next 24 hours to experiment with this chapter?

5. How might you sabotage or resist experimenting, with baby steps, for more adventure in your life (look for information, in this book, that can help to release resistance with <u>The Ten Step Miracle</u> or <u>Bio-spiritual Focusing</u>)?

6. What type of additional support might you need to help transform daily life into an amazingly adventurous life? Like- minded friends, groups, a mentor or sponsor? Your own "inner allies" (as explained in this book) or listening to a "Higher Wisdom" by various means?

Make a quick list if you like.

**Further Notes, Thoughts
Or Ideas**

"Our response to an event
  is more important
  than the event itself."

— *Angeles Arrien*

CHAPTER 13

"Fortune, Misfortune Very Hard to Tell" –

The Amazing Adventure of Adversity

As unlikely as it may seem, adversity can sometimes be the source of life's most positive and beneficial adventures. If we can alter our perceptions of adversity as only being negative, we become open to the possibility that something good could result from our misfortunes. Perhaps the insight of an old Taoist fable captures this idea the best.

A Taoist Fable

A wise old farmer had a very unruly and irresponsible son. One day the wild son went out to the corral to feed the family horse. However, he left the corral gate open and the horse fled out of the gate and ran away. When the man next door heard what happened, he came to visit his neighbor and said, "That crazy son of yours has let your horse run away and now you will not be able to plow your fields or harvest your crops. What a terrible misfortune." Calmly, the father of the unruly son replied, "Fortune or misfortune, very hard to tell."

The next day the horse returned home, bringing three wild horses with it. Again, the man next door came over and said, "Who would believe it? That crazy son of yours let your only horse run away, and now you have four horses. You will be able to plant more than ever, sell what you don't need for yourself and make a large profit. How fortunate you are!" The father said calmly again, "Fortune or misfortune, very hard to tell."

A few days later, the unreliable boy went out to the corral again and tried to ride one of the wild horses. The horse threw him off and he broke his leg. The man next door came over again and said, "How sad, now your crazy son will not be able to help you in the fields and you may not be able to grow enough food to last through next winter. What a misfortune." The wise, old father said again, "Fortune or misfortune, very hard to tell."

The following day, the army came to their village to enlist all the young men to go off to war against a neighboring country. When the army officers came to the farmhouse of the unruly son and saw his broken leg, they said, "He is a reject." and they proceeded on to the next farm. Soon, the neighbor returned and said, "This is unbelievable. All of our sons are gone to fight in the war and, after your son gets well, you'll be the only one in the village to have help in plowing and planting your fields. You are so incredibly fortunate." The father answered softly, "Fortune or misfortune, very hard to tell."

The Lesson

What is the wisdom in this story? What we thought was bad can sometimes turn out to be good. Similarly, what we may think is an unfortunate event or mishap in our lives today can sometimes turn out to be the source of a positive, unplanned, new adventure. These kinds of unexpected adventures often lead to experiences that end up being of great value to us. Of course, this isn't always the case. There can be no denying that tragic events do happen in life which cause much pain and suffering. The adventure into our spiritual depths which often accompanies this kind of pain and suffering is certainly not a welcome form of adventure. Even in tragedy, however, a higher level of Wisdom may one day become the source of new spiritual insight in this adventure of life on earth.

Turning Lemons Into Lemonade

An excellent example of finding adventure within adversity is the story of what happened to the co-author of this book, Richard, while on a brief trip with his son. After a full day of travel and recreational activity, the first order of business was to find a place to stay for the night. That's when they discovered that every hotel in town, for no apparent reason, was occupied. Instead of considering their plight a major disaster, they decided to make it an unplanned, spontaneous adventure. They decided the first thing they would do is have a nice leisurely dinner and go to a late movie.

Next, they found an all-night bowling alley where they could bowl as long as they wanted without crowds or disruptions of any kind. It was this night that Richard bowled his best game ever. This was followed by riding their bikes (which, of course, they brought with them) around the lighted bowling alley parking lot. Shortly before dawn, they decided to look for an all-night coffee shop and have an early breakfast. In the morning, they were able to get a room at one of the larger hotels in the area and slept half way through the day. This unexpected adventure turned out to be the highlight of their trip. Richard and his son (as the saying goes) "turned lemons into lemonade"—which is the central idea of finding adventure in adversity.

Practice: Shifting Misfortune Into Fortune

1. Make a list of several common possible mishaps, adverse circumstances or major inconveniences which you could encounter at some future time (anything from a flat tire to catching a cold, missing your airline connection or even being laid off at work, etc.).
2. Decide on the first thing you would do to take care of the problem in each of these situations.
3. Next, decide what you would do in each situa-

tion to make it easier to take care of yourself.

4. Now, think of one or two possible ways in which each of these situations could end up being fortunate and become an unplanned adventure.

5. Use this process in deciding how to handle and respond to other adverse situations in the future. It can greatly reduce our fear of the unknown and open the way to confidently turning adversity into adventure.

About This Chapter

Here are six suggestions or six action steps or six questions to help transform the ideas in this chapter into A **Really Radical Spiritually Adventurous Life**. *Write your responses on these pages just as if this were a workbook or on a separate sheet of paper (if you prefer privacy, may want to loan the book to someone, etc.).*

1. What caught your attention or was of particular interest to you in this chapter?

2. Any new ideas or possible adventures you might want to think about after reading this chapter?

3. What have you not thought about that this chapter has brought to your attention?

4. What would be one small step you could do in the next 24 hours to experiment with this chapter?

5. How might you sabotage or resist experimenting, with baby steps, for more adventure in your life (look for information, in this book, that can help to release resistance with _The Ten Step Miracle_ or _Bio-spiritual Focusing_)?

6. What type of additional support might you need to help transform daily life into an amazingly adventurous life? Like- minded friends, groups, a mentor or sponsor? Your own "inner allies" (as explained in this book) or listening to a "Higher Wisdom" by various means?

Make a quick list if you like.

**Further Notes, Thoughts
Or Ideas**

"Spiritual literacy is the ability to read the text of our lives for sacred meaning."

— *Mary Ann Brussat*

Treasuring Our Journey —
A Healing Adventure of Making Past Hurts Go Away

What on earth have you been doing? Having a clear answer to that question can give us a wonderful sense of wholeness and confidence. Being able to see, at any given point in time, how we got to where we are today can also be very satisfying and reassuring. There is a simple way to portray the earlier events of our lives, no matter how difficult some of them may have been, as positive and valuable adventures to be remembered and treasured.

The purpose of this chapter is to recommend making a picture album which tells a positive, chronological story of our lives from birth to the present. Using old photographs and pictures cut out of old magazines (available from used book stores), we can create a portrayal of what was positive in the events of our past. We can depict these good things as valuable past adventures in our lives worth honoring and remembering. Seeing life's journey laid out before us in a positive way gives us a great sense of continuity we may have never known before. It can even have a spiritual quality.

Rewriting Our History

Creating an album of what on earth we've been doing can be a surprising adventure in itself. Because we are now deliberately deciding what was good and valuable in our past, we are taking control over rewriting and reframing our history. We suddenly become the author of our lives, which can be very transforming and healing. Turning these past events of our lives into a series of meaningful adventures is certainly capable of being an adventure all by itself.

Building a Treasure Map

– Begin listing where you've lived in your life and look for pictures of those places or pictures that fit with how it might have looked.

– Look for pictures of clothing styles you liked in the past and items around the house that you liked looking at or enjoyed in some way.

– Think about cars or pets or other specific things in the past that you liked and look for pictures of them.

– Collect as many photos and pictures of as many people, places and things as you like and organize them year by year.

– Place your collection of photos and pictures into an album in chronological order starting from the earliest time possible. Include only that which feels right. It's okay to skip over certain times or leave things out. You are in charge now.

– Once year or so (or whenever you want), revisit your life journey album and treasure your valuable past adventures.

About This Chapter

Here are six suggestions or six action steps or six questions to help transform the ideas in this chapter into A **Really Radical Spiritually Adventurous Life**. *Write your responses on these pages just as if this were a workbook or on a separate sheet of paper (if you prefer privacy, may want to loan the book to someone, etc.).*

1. What caught your attention or was of particular interest to you in this chapter?

2. Any new ideas or possible adventures you might want to think about after reading this chapter?

3. What have you not thought about that this chapter has brought to your attention?

4. What would be one small step you could do in the next 24 hours to experiment with this chapter?

5. How might you sabotage or resist experimenting, with baby steps, for more adventure in your life (look for information, in this book, that can help to release resistance with <u>The Ten Step Miracle</u> or <u>Bio-spiritual Focusing</u>)?

6. What type of additional support might you need to help transform daily life into an amazingly adventurous life? Like- minded friends, groups, a mentor or sponsor? Your own "inner allies" (as explained in this book) or listening to a "Higher Wisdom" by various means?

Make a quick list if you like.

**Further Notes, Thoughts
Or Ideas**

"Youth is a circumstance you can't do anything about. The trick is to grow up without growing old."

— Frank Lloyd Wright

CHAPTER 15

The Truth About Aging Gracefully –
It Can Be a Profound Adventure If..

From the moment we are born, we begin to die—we are aging. In fact, most of the cells in our bodies die and are replaced many times over during our lifetime. The average lifespan in 1917 was 47 years. Now it's 77 years—a thirty year jump. This is the largest increase in longevity in the entire history of man, and it's due largely to advances in medical science, sanitation, and food production.

The adventure of aging gracefully challenges our generation to use this 30 year jump in longevity so that our last years are not filled with pain, loss of memory, depression and isolation. This adventure requires us to advance the quality of life and do our best so that we age with renewed vigor, passion, and aliveness.

New research is exploding the myths and false

beliefs about aging. Only recently, it was believed that as we grow older, we must accept that we will gradually lose our ability to remember, move about or work effectively. Just as racism and sexism have limited our society, age discrimination continues to influence our ideas about aging gracefully. Cliches persist, such as "You're pushing 40", "Over the hill at 50" and so on. Forced retirements were commonplace, deeming a certain age as the end of a productive life.

But a new era of healthy aging has begun. We do not have to age like most of our parents or grandparents.

Retrain the Brain

Arnold Sheibel is a robust 81-year-old professor of microbiology and psychology at the University of California Los Angeles and former director of the Brain Research Institute. His research on the brain proves that neurons and their interconnections can remain remarkably plastic into our 80's and beyond. New neurological pathways can be found or rerouted around older, more rigid areas. "The brain remains plastic until death. With plasticity we can short-circuit evolution. We can force ourselves to evolve within our own lifetime." The University of California—which employs Dr. Sheibel—has thrown out its previous mandatory age requirements for retirement. More and more, as the large and powerful baby boomer population becomes seniors or elders, institutions are recognizing that age does not equal the end of a productive, fulfilling life.

Deepok Chopra, M.D. reports dramatic evidence supported by research that physical aspects of aging can be altered by the mind. Dr. Marian Diamond's groundbreaking research in the 1960's proves that mental stimulation or new learning can stimulate and improve the immune system: "Mental stimulation prolongs life." Even physically frail elderly stay healthy when they stimulate their minds with games, puzzles, and other intellectual pursuits.

So, if you're moving into mid-life and think you're losing it—mentally and physically—just wait a minute. My own family members debunk the myths of the physical and mental debilitation of growing older. My father wrote four novels after age 80 and died at age 91. He considered this period to be the best time of his life. My grandparents both lived to be 101 years old after having worked full time cutting men and women's hair in their wonderful beauty salon until they were 95. They followed intuitively what research is proving today: One's lifestyle—heart, body, mind and soul—is they key to a high quality and long life.

In a famous longevity study, Swedish doctors studied 10,000 pairs of twins. They found that a long and good quality life was influenced only one-third by a person's genetics. The majority of influence can be attributed to practicing a healthy lifestyle of balancing nutritious food, physical fitness and mental stimulation.

Besides my own family members who have lived a healthy lifestyle, there are other famous role models for longevity. Grandma Moses started painting at age 80 and continued to live a robust life. Frank Lloyd Wright, the great architect, was most prolific from ages 80 to 93 (when he died).

Working the Mind "Muscles"

Yes, genetics are a factor we cannot control, although stem cell research and genetic engineering may even change that. What we *can* influence is our willingness to live a lifestyle balancing the elements of heart, body, mind and soul.

First, we can use our minds and maintain mental alertness and memory by using the following steps:

1. Find and follow our passions or callings in life.

2. Set specific goals, such as 30 things to do before death.

3. Overcome self-limiting beliefs about aging.

4. Become a life-long learner.

5. Assert your truth and speak up.

David Halberstom wrote "The greatest test of aging gracefully with mental alertness is do you still get excited about what you do when you get up in the morning?"

Dr. Paul Missbaum states if we continue to learn, it is like a vaccination against late life degenerative diseases of the brain. Learning new languages, piano, other music lessons, or really anything you love, will actually stimulate brain functions and our immune system.

Remember?

Included in mental fitness is memory. Any aging person can be concerned about memory and memory loss. Yet, just because you are getting older doesn't automatically mean you will become overly forgetful; we are much more absent-minded at age five. Think about it. It's not abnormal to forget where you put your keys, but it IS if you forget what those keys are used for. Samuel Jackson, a noted expert on memory, stated "We consider ourselves as defective in memory either because we remember less than we desire or less than we suppose others to remember." In other words, we compare and judge ourselves too harshly.

New to the real issue of memory loss is our ability to focus, concentrate, or pay attention at any age. My 21 year old son walked into the kitchen and forgot why and what he was looking for. I've seen my other teenagers forget things for school, while I've seen an 85 year old woman remember to go to her weekly bridge meeting. You don't automatically become forgetful as you get older—it's just a matter of keeping your memory functioning. In fact, by practicing tools for focus and concentration, you can even improve your memory over time.

Cicero states, "I've never heard of an old man (or woman) who forgot where their money was hidden." Dr. Bruce Whittlesea, psychology professor at Simon Fraser University, has studied memory for 20 years and asserts "The key to good memory is interest."

The following six areas are the most troublesome areas of forgetfulness:

1. People's names
2. Important dates and appointments
3. Location of household items
4. Recent or past events
5. To take vitamins and medications
6. Important information and facts

...Yes, NOW I Remember!

So how do you improve your memory? Choose one or two areas that you would like to improve and practice the following ideas. In all six areas, slow down, pay attention, observe and be gentle with yourself. It's normal in our busy, information-packed world to have difficulty remembering.

People's Names. As soon as the name is stated, repeat it out loud or say "How do you do, Bill (name of person)". Also mentally associate the name with anything or anyone. For example, Julie with jewelry could be a connection.

Important dates and appointments. You can make lists, use a calendar or daily journal or a pocket computer to remember these things. Review your schedule at the same time every day to help remember important dates or appointments.

Locating household items. Learn to organize

these items. Hang your keys in the same place. Have a special pocket or purse for important items. Make special drawers for each category of items. "A place for everything and everything in its place."

Remembering past events. If you wish to remember a recent or past event, the key is to give it emotional interest. You will remember what interests you, if you want to remember. Pay attention and focus. It's your choice. Or *don't* pay attention. It's okay not to remember if it's not important to you.

Taking vitamins and other medications. Again, the key is organization. Have them in clear sight to remind you. Obtain a daily, weekly, or monthly container.

Important information and facts. Learn to make a mental note where you parked your car or where you put your keys. Write down information in a small notebook you carry with you. Put it in your calendar or computer. Don't use scraps of paper that you may lose—have a special spot. And if you forget, don't blame yourself. At every age we forget things. Forgive yourself and keep practicing.

So, now pick one or two areas to experiment with this next week. Which areas will give you the most benefit? Have fun learning to improve—at any age!

About This Chapter

Here are six suggestions or six action steps or six questions to help transform the ideas in this chapter into A **Really Radical Spiritually Adventurous Life**. *Write your responses on these pages just as if this were a workbook or on a separate sheet of paper (if you prefer privacy, may want to loan the book to someone, etc.).*

1. What caught your attention or was of particular interest to you in this chapter?

2. Any new ideas or possible adventures you might want to think about after reading this chapter?

3. What have you not thought about that this chapter has brought to your attention?

4. What would be one small step you could do in the next 24 hours to experiment with this chapter?

5. How might you sabotage or resist experimenting, with baby steps, for more adventure in your life (look for information, in this book, that can help to release resistance with _The Ten Step Miracle_ or _Bio-spiritual Focusing_)?

6. What type of additional support might you need to help transform daily life into an amazingly adventurous life? Like- minded friends, groups, a mentor or sponsor? Your own "inner allies" (as explained in this book) or listening to a "Higher Wisdom" by various means?

Make a quick list if you like.

**Further Notes, Thoughts
Or Ideas**

"There are two ways to live:
you can live as if nothing is
a miracle; you can live as if
everything is a miracle."

— *Albert Einstein*

CHAPTER **16**

The Ultimate Adventure:
Befriending The End of This Human Experience

When I was growing up, I was given two competing views of death. One belief from my parents through our Catholic faith was that I had an eternal soul which would live in the hereafter in "Heaven" if I were a good person. (If I was just behaving so-so, I would go to an in-between place called "limbo"). If I were really bad, I would die with a mortal sin on my soul; I would go to "Hell"—a very bad place.

There was another view I obtained later in high school from friends and in college. This notion had that if this life was "it", this form of my body aging and decaying would eventually die and I would be nothing. So I had better enjoy life and get all I can before I die because this is "it". These competing views are better known as eternalism and nihilism, respectively.

191

Neither of these views or beliefs gave me much comfort. Waiting for the judgment day based on being good or bad did not release my fear or dread of dying. I held on to eternalism because at least it felt better than nihilism, which left me in even more despair, giving me a point of view of turning into dust without meaning while trying to gain quick fix pleasures and avoid pain. Oh yes, the silver lining in nihilism was that I could create my own meaning and purpose of a higher order and *then* turn into dust. With this idea I'd probably be happier while living; but neither notion comforted my continued dread of dying. My fear of dying was not of physical death as much as the fear of losing my sense of self, who I am, "Richard Lui", my story and memories. This was a feeling of abandonment or separation, fear of being alone, as well as a fear of the unknown or nothingness.

The Illusion of Separation

The fear of death masquerades itself underneath other fears, that we all have, either conscious or unconscious. Most humans are afraid of being rejected or not being approved of. Underneath this fear is a primal fear of being alone or separate and even physical death. We obtain this fear early in life, maybe in the baby crib when our parents are not there , and we cry out for connection. When mom or dad comes, we are soothed. We feel belonging, connection, and love. Later as we grow, we might mess up, bring home bad grades or fight with our siblings, and our parents might overact and shame us, calling our behavior bad. In a child's black and white thinking, when we are punished, we take it personally. "I'm bad." "I'm a mistake," instead of "I made a mistake." Under this "I'm bad" is "Nobody loves me. If nobody loves me they might leave me, discard me as worthless and unlovable. I'm alone, I might die." This latter is more often felt in the unconscious rather than thought of consciously.

We have inherited this fear of death from our tribal ancestors and the genetics of trying to stay alive and loved by the group. To be rejected in early human tribal culture meant being ostracized and removed from the tribe, often leading to death. The fear of death and separation was used by rulers and those in power to keep the peasants conforming and safely under their thumb.

While the fears of physical death or being alone keeps us somewhat safe in our collective, conforming to the tribe's or society's wishes, an excessive fear keeps us hyper-vigilant and fearing the future and wounds us. It keeps us from our innate happiness of living in the precious present and enjoying the now—the only moment we can be happy. Other than a moderate fear of death leading to a concern for one's welfare, an excessive worrying or fear of anything in the future removes the ability to be happy right now. Old fears and traumas from the past based on abandonment and separation in childhood can keep us stuck in the past and projecting the same fears into the future.

Thus the underlying fears or wounding are connected to a fear of death, of not belonging, and the story of "If I am alone, then I am not wanted or loved. I must be worthless."

Suspend Your Concepts

So what are we to do? However comforting, our notions of eternalism and nihilism are only band-aid beliefs to help comfort these fears of the future and the trauma of past. They do not deeply assure or experientially allow us to feel actually comforted because they are concepts of the mind and must be taken on faith because others have told us so.

For a few minutes, I would request that you suspend whichever notions about death you have learned—eternalism, nihilism, or some other concept. 2,600 years ago, the Buddha told an interesting parable about ideas of notions. A tradesman came home to see that robbers had kidnapped his young son and burned down his home. Outside the home was the charred body of a small person. The tradesman thought this was his son, not realizing the robbers had taken his child before burning the house down. His grief was huge. His entire life revolved around the love of his young son. To comfort himself, the father, upon his son's cremation, put his son's ashes in a small velvet bag and carried them wherever he went, weeping and crying. One night his son escaped from the robbers and ran home late at night to the new home his father had built. He knocked on the door, excitedly yelling out to his father, "It is me, your son." His father yelled back, not opening the door, "Bad child, go away. My son died three months ago; go away. I have his ashes right here with me." The son cried and cried, pounding on the door to be let in, but to no avail. Finally, he left to never return. The father held on to the ashes and his belief, and lost his son forever.

The Buddha taught that if you get caught in an idea and dogmatically hold it as the truth, you too will be closed to experiencing the truth. Your door may be closed, even if a person comes knocking to invite you to see and experience your happiness right now. In Buddhism, mindfulness training helps free us from adopting dogmatically any absolute point of view. Dogmatism invites judgment of others and creates fanaticism or "I am right and you're wrong."

A New View of an Old Idea

Buddhism asks us to go beyond ideas and notions, even Buddhist concepts, to meditate deeply and experience the truth directly, the truth that allows an experience of happiness, safety and inner peace now. I invite you to not only love a notion, but also experience your truth intuitively. Even the Buddhist view of death is a notion unless you allow yourself to inquire deeply and intuitively to feel the truth.

First, the Buddhist view is a middle path between externalism and nihilism. It offers both rational and experiential proof that shows us the opposite of birth is not death but rebirth—that nothing is born nor does it die, it just changes form. The French scientist Lavoisier declared, "Nothing is born, nothing dies." Or, as other scientists state, "Matter can be neither created nor destroyed." He discovered what Buddha discovered, that our true nature is not created, nor can it be destroyed. Once we touch our true nature, we transcend our fear of separation, death or annihilation, or being alone.

So our greatest fear is that we were born from nothing and that when we die, we will become nothing.

The Buddha gave another understanding of the false idea we come from nothing, live a life span, and die and go to nothing, creating a deep fear and suffering. These are illusions based on faulty thinking. If we look deeply at the nature of all things—there is no birth or death. Everything is changing moment to moment, being born again, dying, changing into a new form—manifesting into new forms, but still part of the whole part of life. There is no material permanency and therefore there is no annihilation. Once we see deeply that we never die, we are free, relieved of this fear of becoming nothing. Our little selves are connected to a greater self called life or God. We think we are separate, not connected to anything outside ourselves. With this faulty thinking, we are scared to lose ourselves—we again fear death. When we know we are part of everything and we are interconnected with all forms—our form will change and become another—then we know there is no fear and no death, only rebirth. The only permanency is an abiding loving Awareness that watches all these changes, life to death and rebirth. We have this ability to watch ourselves and others with great compassion and love. With this compassionate love, we can even embrace our fears as everything changes within and around us.

For instance, pull out a photo of yourself when you were little. Are you still that child of long ago? Yes, you are the same, and you are different. Every cell of your body has changed. Many of your emotions and beliefs and ideas have changed, died and been reborn into new emotional cognitive formations. And at the same time you are the same person. You are an ancestor to yourself. In the DNA of you as a child is accumulated the physical memory of all your ancestors as well. So your body is really a continuation from your ancestors and is now continuing into your children and will continue into theirs.

In a paradoxical way, your body is not really your body. It is your own and part of a greater whole continuing and changing. If you identify with your body like, "I'm okay if I'm young and healthy," then you will suffer more as your body ages, grows older and dies. Your body is made up mostly of water, oxygen, carbons and other minerals. It is interconnected with all other plant, rock and animal cells in a larger self called life. If you are willing, you can connect to your own loving witness in meditation and begin the journey of accepting your aging with joy and grieving the inevitable body changes as we age and die to this body.

Everything is Connected

Remember a time when you walked or sat happily at a sunset or sunrise in your garden and felt that connection—the peace, security, happiness at experiencing that connection.

The paper you are reading right now has a history before its birth into paper. It has been a tree, and before that the sun, and before that a cloud or rain and soil and minerals. And before that, part of the cosmos. If you look deeply into this paper, you might still see the clouds, the trees and the cosmos. If you look deeply you can see that this sheet of paper has never died and will be reborn again and again. If you took away one part of the paper, say the sunshine, the sheet of paper would not have manifested. Or if you take away the trees, there could be no paper. This is why the sunshine and trees are in the paper—look deeply and see their continuation. See how you, too, are impermanent and have changed forms even within your own lifespan as you see your own self as a child. See how you are part of a greater whole in the cosmos like the paper and all of its ancestors.

Stop and Witness Yourself

Stop for a while, cease running anxiously, fearing rejection, fearing not belonging, fearing being alone and separate. Stop waiting to be happy if you succeed and have money in the future. Feel deeply how you're connected to a greater self called life. You are life itself. There is nothing wrong with success or money, but if it is out of balance with enjoying the now—your fear of death is causing you to suffer.

When you pause and enjoy the moment and see deeply that you are not going to die—you were not ever born (from nothing)—every moment becomes a new moment to be reborn in this lifetime and whatever form your body takes as it ages. Don't wait to be reborn until you die from this body. Every moment is a chance to be reborn and to touch your true nature and see deeply your loving connection to everyone and everything around you. If you live these principles, you would argue less with your parents or children or spouse. Love them now as they are in their present form because they are changing and impermanent. When they die, grieve their loss, but know they are still here in you, around you.

When my father died at age 91 a few years ago, his body form had aged and withered. He was cremated and buried with my mother's ashes at Arlington National Cemetery. But my father lives on in me and in my children. The fruits of his life are living on in this book. He told me by his words and actions to write books and enjoy the process. The book you are reading is a continuation of him and his influence. Thank you, Dad.

You don't have to wait until you die to release the fear and suffering of death, dying and annihilation. Through the practice of mindfulness—of being present in the moment with gratitude to what you have and are today—this will bring you to your inner connectedness.

Thich Nhat Hanh, the great Buddhist monk, advises us to practice the now. He notes that if we are fearful as we age and die, or if we believe that our body is who we are, we will suffer in the now. Life becomes a living hell. But it is possible to live happily and die peacefully.

Unbounded Living, Unbounded Joy

Live each day as if it is your last.

Enjoy each moment. See your impermanent nature. See how you are connected to all forms. See how your body is just a form, a vehicle, that is changing and impermanent but connected to all life. When your form dies, you will be reborn like the paper and its ancestors.

So if we practice detaching from our bodies—that not only are we our bodies, but our true nature is beyond our bodies—if we practice, our suffering will ease now and at the time of our deaths. Thich Nhat Hanh advised to practice the following meditation:

> "These eyes are not me. I am not caught in my eyes. I am life without boundaries." (Hanh 1993)

Or close your eyes, imagine the next breath as if it were the first and feel the wonder, then take another breath and imagine it is your last in this body as you transcend into the mystery and deep peace of a larger body called life or love of God. The source without a name...deep peace without boundaries. If this last breath brings up tears, just embrace the baby fear as a mother would a child. It's okay to feel afraid. Fear can release as you slowly learn to embrace it as the child within that needs and wants to be held. As it is held, the fear slowly turns into excitement and maybe even openness to beauty, awe and wonder of your transition into another form of the great mystery called life.

No Fear, No Death is an ongoing practice. Practice having a happy death now, so when you actually die, you will take these deep truths with you.

About This Chapter

Here are six suggestions or six action steps or six questions to help transform the ideas in this chapter into A **Really Radical Spiritually Adventurous Life**. Write your responses on these pages just as if this were a workbook or on a separate sheet of paper (if you prefer privacy, may want to loan the book to someone, etc.).

1. What caught your attention or was of particular interest to you in this chapter?

2. Any new ideas or possible adventures you might want to think about after reading this chapter?

3. What have you not thought about that this chapter has brought to your attention?

4. What would be one small step you could do in the next 24 hours to experiment with this chapter?

5. How might you sabotage or resist experimenting, with baby steps, for more adventure in your life (look for information, in this book, that can help to release resistance with _The Ten Step Miracle_ or _Bio-spiritual Focusing_)?

6. What type of additional support might you need to help transform daily life into an amazingly adventurous life? Like- minded friends, groups, a mentor or sponsor? Your own "inner allies" (as explained in this book) or listening to a "Higher Wisdom" by various means?

Make a quick list if you like.

Further Notes, Thoughts
Or Ideas

"There is no cure for
birth and death
save to enjoy the interval."

— *George Santayana*

Bibliography

Alcoholics Anonymous, Fourth Edition. New York: Alcoholics Anonymous World Services, Inc., 2001.

Gendlin, Eugene. *Focusing*. New York: Bantam, 1981.

Hanh, Thich Nhat. *No Fear, No Death*. New York: Riverhead Books, 2002.

Hister, Art. *Dr. Art Hister's Guide to Living a Long & Healthy Life*. Vancouver: Greystone Books, 2005.

McMahm, Edwin and Campbell, Peter *Biospirituality, Focusing As a Way to Grow (2002)*

About The Authors

Richard Lui

Richard Lui, M.S., MFT, is a licensed individual, couple and family therapist and hypnotherapist in private practice for the last 30 years in Sacramento, California.

Richard loves everyday adventures on his own, with his wife and with his three now grown children Aaron, Allison and Megan. He passionately practices all the adventures included in this book.

In addition, Richard teaches many courses at Adult Community Centers and at the Learning Exchange in Sacramento, Sierra College, Rocklin and at Always Learning in Elk Grove, CA.

His career adventures include law school student, elementary school teacher and school psychologist.

"Live a life of adventure" is his motto.

Jim Regan

Bringing a spirit of adventure into everyday life has

taken Jim in numerous professional directions. A graduate of Arizona State University, Jim began his career as a social worker in the Phoenix area. Moving to San Francisco some years later, Jim joined the airline industry to develop and conduct quality control and efficiency surveys and other industrial psychology activities. In this position, Jim traveled extensively.

Following his years with the airlines, an opportunity to work in the public sector came next. There Jim continued to provide psychological and industrial engineering studies and surveys for the Department of Defense.

Then, in the spirit of true adventure, Jim's next move took him into Nevada's resort hotel business. Here he provided supervisory and consultant services to the Nevada-style entertainment community.

Now residing in Sacramento, California, Jim continues the adventure of making everyday a new discovery with the help of the ideas and concepts set forth in this book. Jim is a board certified clinical hypnosis therapist and an internationally published author.

For additional copies of this book,

To obtain information for individual or group counseling regarding any of these great adventures,

To be placed on a mailing list for future classes or workshops,

Call, write or fax to:

Richard Lui
Life Balance Counseling Center
2740 Fulton Avenue, Suite 118
Sacramento, CA 95821
(916) 481- 0234 (Office)
(916) 481-2230 (FAX)